THE ULTIMATE SCIENCE QUIZ BOOK

THE ULTIMATE SCIENCE QUIZ BOOK

VOLUME 1

Bill G. Aldridge

Illustrated by
Stanislav Lukhin

FRANKLIN WATTS
New York / Chicago / London / Toronto / Sydney

Photographs copyright ©:
Visuals Unlimited: pp. 31 (John D. Cunningham),
42 bottom (R. Kessel–C. V. Shih), 84 (Leonard Lee Rue III);
The Bettmann Archive: p. 42; Comstock/Russ Kinne: p. 85;
Photo Researchers, Inc./Francois Gohier: p.113

Library of Congress Cataloging-in-Publication Data

Aldridge, Bill G.
    The ultimate science quiz book, volume 1 / Bill G. Aldridge.
        p. cm.
    Includes index.
    ISBN 0-531-11198-9 (lib. bdg.)
    1. Science—Experiments—Juvenile literature. [1. Science
    —Experiments. 2. Experiments.] I. Title.
    Q182.3.Q43 1994
    507.8—dc20   94-15518 CIP AC

A little learning is a Dangerous thing;
Drink deep, or taste not the Pierian spring:
There shallow droughts intoxicate the brain,
And drinking largely sobers us again.

Alexander Pope
"Essay on Criticism" (l711)

C O N T E N T S

ACKNOWLEDGMENTS

This book resulted almost entirely from the stimulation, inspiration, and prodding of two people.

One was Dr. Linda Crow, project director for the Scope, Sequence, and Coordination Project, Division of School Based Programs, of Houston's Baylor College of Medicine. For a long time I expressed frustration to many of my colleagues about how we might show what is meant by depth of understanding in science. It seemed impossible to do so with general outlines or descriptions. In the course of these discussions, Dr. Crow suggested that we do it through well-designed quiz items, items that could not have simple or short answers. She then suggested the van Helmont experiment as a source for one such question.

Not only did this book result in part from Dr. Crow's suggestion about van Helmont's experiment; with Dr. Russel Aiuto, the three of us wrote a separate monograph on photosynthesis (referenced in this book). I would like to thank Dr. Crow for having stimulated these activities, and for her additional suggestions and comments about the draft of the book.

The other person who clearly was responsible for this book's being written was Mr. Tom Cohn, Senior Editor at Franklin Watts. Mr. Cohn had seen a few sample items of the kind we were trying to write. He suggested that such items might make a book. He asked that I consider preparing such a book for Franklin Watts. I must confess that I did not take the suggestion seriously enough, and therefore did little initially to respond to Mr. Cohn's suggestion. However, he was persistent. His persistence eventually paid off, and I agreed to write the book.

My gratitude goes to both Linda Crow and Tom Cohn for their stimulation, inspiration, prodding, help, comments, and advice. I like the book that resulted, and I hope you do too.

THE ULTIMATE SCIENCE QUIZ BOOK

This book has been titled *The Ultimate Science Quiz Book*. What is this book, and why was it written? Who is it for?

Too much of what we all learned or are learning in school consists of facts, terminology, and memorization. Because teachers use tests to obtain grades, they too often teach what is easy to test. Such learning is not much fun, and it is not very interesting. Perhaps this is because it is so difficult to test for real depth of understanding of concepts, principles, and laws of science.

One of the major barriers to learning science is the fact that so much of what you learn is provided in detailed exposition or explanation. Well-illustrated books, beautifully crafted videos, or well-designed computer simulations do little to help you learn, although they can be engrossing or even entertaining. You learn best by interacting with, and thinking about, the subject under study.

Problems, puzzles, questions, and the like challenge you, and they are often interesting to solve or answer. It is through *your own efforts* that you learn science concepts, principles, laws, and theories. Most often the learning occurs as you struggle to solve a problem.

Science textbooks contain so much, in the way of facts, concepts, empirical laws, theories of science, and especially applications to our technology, it is difficult for the person learning science to sort out what is most important to learn and remember. What is really basic? And what do you really need to learn that will enable you to solve a wide range of problems or understand complex issues having scientific components?

Mostly, you need skepticism. You should always ask why. And you must resist the natural tendency to feel uncomfortable asking questions. You do not want to appear to know less than others, who may not be asking such questions. But if the truth were known, you would find that they do not understand either. If a person does not know *why* something is true, or *how we know* something is true, then that person does not understand it. If someone else can tell something about science to you, but cannot explain why or how he or she knows, then you should be suspicious of that knowledge.

Nature has a wonderful way of testing our knowledge. Nature provides the ultimate test. Whatever the books say, or whatever your teachers or others who might be in authority say, unsupported assertions mean nothing if nature does not agree. Your test of nature is through careful observation and experiment. It is a remarkable fact that two quite independent observers can "test" nature and get the same results, from which they may also come to the same conclusions.

Conclusions drawn from observations or experiments often involve interpretations, and interpretations require theories or models. This is where science is most fun—creating new theories. There can be alternative explanations. One theory is just as good as another, unless it makes *new* predictions that are confirmed, while the other theory does not make any new predictions.

Often, students are not taught the differences among facts, concepts, empirical laws, or theories. Nor are they taught to apply their knowledge of science to practical problems. This is in part because of the problem of testing. The barrier that prevents us from testing for deep understanding of science is that such tests are very difficult to prepare. They are difficult to score or grade. The easiest tests are those that ask for simple, one-word answers, or for responses to multiple-choice items. But such tests almost never measure depth of understanding.

In this book, you will notice that the answers are almost always longer and even more detailed than the questions. This is the nature of *real science. Important questions in science seldom have short answers.*

You will also notice that most items in this book are most often *quantitative*. This is because depth of understanding of science is seldom present if a person does not understand the quantitative aspects. This point was made best, perhaps, by Lord Kelvin (1824–1907), when he said in a lecture delivered on May 3, 1883:

> When you can measure what you are speaking about, and express it in numbers, you know something about it; but when you cannot measure it, when you cannot express it in numbers, your knowledge is of a meagre and unsatisfactory kind.

This book is an attempt to offer the person who is curious about science, and motivated to learn about it, an opportunity to test his or her understanding in much greater depth. The book is intended for use by people of all ages. Although upon first glance it may appear difficult, very little of the book is highly abstract or particularly difficult. Scientific inquiry and the questions in this book (unlike many tests administered by teachers) are not *closed-book* tests. Readers should feel free to make use of textbooks, reference books, trade books, and any other source of information. The very exceptional person in one of the disciplines will find that the items in his or her area of specialty are not too difficult. But it will be a very rare person who can manage easily to solve problems in all of the various science disciplines represented in the book.

Many of the items in this quiz book have interesting applications to real life. Others have profound implications in terms of the fundamentals of science. Thus, if you can successfully answer these quiz items without help, and without looking first at the answers, that is an admirable and important achievement.

Some of the items in this quiz can be used as starting points for research for student competitions like science fairs, Westinghouse Scholarships or other such competitions, or further reading by teachers or other adults interested in science.

Solutions to some items give the reader a deeper and more comprehensive understanding of the world in which he or she lives. Others are stimulating, are interesting, or will give you new ideas for research, experimentation, or observation. The annotated bibliography at the end of each chapter tells you where to look for more detailed reading material on the particular items in that chapter, or on related areas of interest.

Although the author has tried to create original and unique quiz items, there is very little new under the sun. Many of the ideas for items have been around for decades. Bright people in science regularly exchange such ideas in intellectual challenges to one another. Some items are completely new and have never before appeared in any form anywhere. A few items are classic, in one form or another, and everyone in that field of science has heard of them. The best example of such items is the one in which you are asked how to measure the height of a building with a mercury barometer. The author first heard it from Dr. Alexander Calandra, a physics professor at Washington University in St. Louis, in the early 1960s.

This book is intended to challenge your mind. It is not expected that you should find a solution to an item easily or quickly. Some solutions may come easily; others may take a long time, with many false starts and mistakes. But *these* are the kinds of items that teach you the most. You will learn more science through such false starts, errors, and mistakes, than in getting items correct on the first try. Indeed, in the latter case, you will learn nothing new.

All test items are subject to interpretation. The author learned long ago that when he thinks that he has a perfectly clear item, someone can always find a different way to interpret it. The reader is therefore urged to accommodate the author and accept the interpretation conveyed by the "answer." But the author would also greatly appreciate hearing from those who have seen a different interpretation, or who have found a better or more interesting solution to the item, or to the reinterpretation.

In spite of our best efforts, there will also be errors. Finding such errors often requires unusual understanding, although all of us can make obvious mistakes. Tell us about these as well. Just write to the author, Bill Aldridge, care of Franklin Watts, 95 Madison Avenue, New York, NY 10016.

CHAPTER 1

THE GREEN MACHINES

WITHOUT PLANTS, life as we know it on earth would not be the same. Plants exchange oxygen and carbon dioxide with all living things; they provide humans with food, shade, essential drugs, and much more. We tend to take plants for granted, and few of us realize their critical contribution to our very survival.

The following items focus on certain important characteristics of green plants. See how much you know about plants—the green machines!

■Q 1.1 Sun Worshipers.

In 1693 John Ray investigated an interesting property of plants. The plants would grow in such a way that they would always end up facing the sun (Figure 1-1).

When a plant has grown while oriented in a certain way, the stem will be bent in a direction that allows the green leaves to gather the most sunlight. If you then turn the plant around, so that the leaves are bent away from the sunlight, the plant will, after some length of time, slowly bend back, becoming vertical and then bending back over again toward the sunlight.

This phenomenon was given the name *heliotropism.* What hypothesis would you offer to account for this movement? What do you think happens inside the plant that can explain this bending? Design an experiment that would

Figure 1-1

allow you to test your hypothesis. What observations and/or measurements would you make?

1.2 Do Plants Eat Soil for Their Food?

A 1.0 gram (g) seed is put into a pot containing 3,129 g of completely dry soil. Water is then added to make the soil moist. The pot is placed where it can receive regular sunshine. Water is added to the soil periodically to maintain precisely the same amount of moisture, and the seed sprouts, producing a green plant (Figure 1-2).

At the end of several months the entire plant, including the roots, is removed from the soil, dried completely, and found to have a mass of 82 g. The soil is also dried completely. Approximately what is the mass of the dry soil at the end of this experiment? How much of the mass that was removed from the original soil was used to provide nutrients or "food" used by the growing plant?

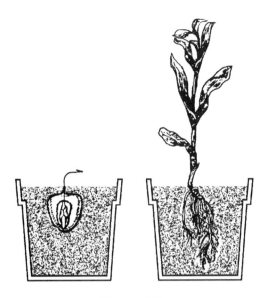

Figure 1-2

Explain in some detail what substances were utilized to form the mass of the plant, and their sources.

■Q 1.3 Gassy Greens.

A green plant with its soil is placed in a clear, uncapped plastic container that has air saturated with water vapor. The plant is placed in a windowsill where it can receive sunshine for several days. One end of a small hose is then attached to a stopper, which seals the container. The other end of this hose is attached to a liquid manometer, so that pressure changes inside the container can be monitored. The liquid in the manometer has a very low vapor pressure, and therefore will not evaporate significantly over the time of this experiment (Figure 1-3).

The container is covered with a dark cloth and kept at a fixed temperature for several days. After that time, the manometer indicates that the pressure inside the container has decreased. How do you explain this phenomenon?

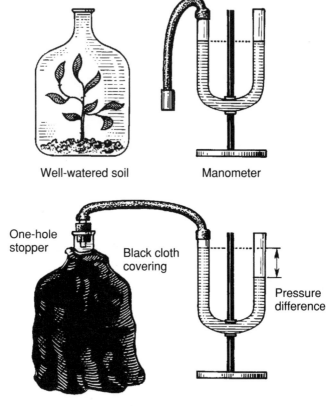

Well-watered soil   Manometer

One-hole stopper

Black cloth covering

Pressure difference

Figure 1-3

■Q **1.4 Leafy Reactions.**

A well-watered green plant was exposed to sunlight for two days. It was then covered with an opaque black cloth for several days. Leaves were then removed, with one third of them subjected to test A, one-third to test B, and one-third to test C.

For tests A and B the leaves were ground up, and water added. In test A, Fehling's solution was added to the water-leaf mixture, and then it was heated. In test B,

Benedict's solution was added to the water-leaf mixture before it was heated. For test C, the leaves were first boiled in water and subsequently placed in warm alcohol. Then they were placed in Lugol's solution.

What did each of these three tests show, and why did we get these results? (If you do not know or remember anything about Fehling's, Benedict's, or Lugol's solutions, you should refer to a biology laboratory textbook or other reference.)

ANSWERS FOR CHAPTER 1

◼A 1.1 Sun Worshipers.

There are two reasonable hypotheses: growth of a plant, with bending of the stem axis toward sunlight, means that the growth of one side of the stem is either being (1) inhibited by something (in this case, in that part of the stem on the illuminated side, the side facing the sun) or (2) promoted by something (in this case, in that part of the stem on the side away from the sun). Such unequal growth of the two sides of the stem would cause the plant to bend toward sunlight. In the case of hypothesis (2), there is a secondary hypothesis: If growth is being promoted in that part of the plant stem on the side of the plant facing away from the sun, whatever the substance is that is promoting this growth must first be produced on the side facing the sun and then somehow transported to the side away from the sun. Both hypotheses assume that there is a substance that either promotes or inhibits cell division and elongation.

The questions to be asked in the design of the experiment are the following: Is there a substance being produced? Where is the substance being produced? How do we know? Since we believe that the sunlight is the stimulus for this effect, curvature must result from something moving down the plant axis, away from the tip or leaves of the plant; it can therefore be assumed that if there is a substance as hypothesized, it is produced in the plant tip. Removing the plant tip and observing that the plant no longer curves toward light illumination of a fixed direction would confirm this assumption.

To test this hypothesis, we could cut off the stem tip of an oat seedling (as done by Frits Went in 1926) that has been kept in light coming from all directions (multidirectional light); the tip is where one would suppose that the substance is being produced. (Figure 1-4).

If no curvature results when the tip is removed, and the plant is exposed to light from a particular direction, the hypothesized substance is being produced at the tip. Next we collect that substance by placing a cut tip from a plant growing in multidirectional light on a block of agar. Some substance is found to move from the tip into the block of

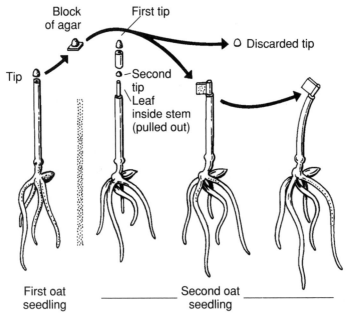

Figure 1-4

agar. A tip is removed from a second oat seedling, and after a short wait, a second tip is removed (in case a new "physiological" tip forms). Suppose next that the block of agar is placed on one side of the stem of the second seedling, and the plant bends to elongate the side on which the substance is concentrated. We would conclude that the substance promotes plant growth on that side of the stem. If the plant bends in the opposite direction, then the substance must inhibit growth on that same side. The results of this experiment show that there is such a substance (called *auxin*) and that it actually promotes the growth of cells (which can be observed with a microscope) on that side of the plant opposite the illumination.

This is basically the experiment performed by Charles Darwin in 1873, as he studied the general phenomenon of phototropism.

■A 1.2 Do Plants Eat Soil for their Food?

This item relates to a common misconception that plants draw "food" from the soil and thereby gain their mass (found in studies of children's misconceptions of science by R. Driver of Leeds, England). Instead, the plant creates, through photosynthesis, solid carbohydrate matter from the synthesis of hydrogen from water and carbon and oxygen from carbon dioxide. The process also synthesizes oxygen from water, and water itself uses excess oxygen from the carbon dioxide and excess hydrogen from the original water. The oxygen from the water is released into the atmosphere.

Not counting the water, the "nutrients" taken from the soil by the plant are almost negligible in mass, although essential to the process. Trace elements are all taken from the soil. The main substance removed from the soil is nitrogen, which, on the average for all green plants, accounts for about 12% of the mass of the dry plant. But some of this nitrogen comes from reactions of water in the soil and nitrogen in the air.

Over several months there will be at most only a few grams of mass lost from the soil itself, even though the dry plant gained a mass of 81 g. Thus the remaining soil, when dried, will have a mass of more than 3,120 g, a loss (mainly associated with nitrogen) of not more than 9 g.

When this experiment was first performed by Jean-Baptiste van Helmont in the early 1600s, he used 200 pounds (lb) of dry soil and a 5-lb willow shoot. After 5 years, the tree weighed 169 lb, but the soil, when dried, had lost only 2 ounces (oz), or about 0.13 lb. This is less than 0.1% of the mass gain of the tree. Not knowing about photosynthesis, van Helmont attributed the mass gain entirely to the water alone. He knew that the tree itself contained a considerable amount of water. Since he did not dry the 169 lb tree, much of its mass was therefore water; had he dried the tree, there still would have remained a very large mass which could not be accounted for by the mass loss of the soil (Figure 1-5).

■A 1.3 Gassy Greens.

During the time the container is in the sunshine, the process of photosynthesis occurs. In this process, carbon dioxide is removed mainly from solution in water vapor, while water is removed from the saturated air and soil. Oxygen and glucose are produced, with the glucose rapidly stored as starch. Even though the container is not sealed, most of the oxygen produced stays in the bottle (since it would take a long time to diffuse out of the small opening in the top of the bottle, especially as the oxygen is continuously produced in sunlight), increasing the interior oxygen concentration relative to that of carbon dioxide.

When the plant's container is capped (and therefore sealed), covered by a dark cloth, and allowed to sit for several days, respiration processes remove oxygen from the interior and produce carbon dioxide. These molecules are exchanged in equal numbers. You would therefore not

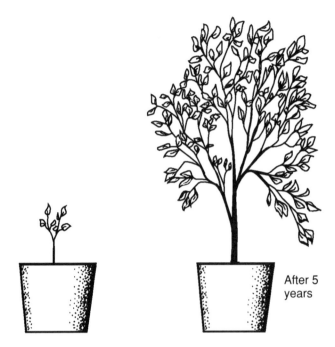

After 5
years

Figure 1-5

expect any change in the pressure. But the pressure inside is observed to decrease.

Even though for each oxygen molecule removed from the interior there is one carbon dioxide molecule produced by respiration, nine times more carbon dioxide than oxygen can be dissolved in a given amount of water. In this situation, the exchange of carbon dioxide and oxygen in the interior of the bottle during respiration is not equal. The fact that a greater number of molecules of carbon dioxide than oxygen dissolve in water creates that imbalance. Thus there is a net loss of "air" molecules from the interior of the container.

The fact that the air inside is saturated with water vapor does not help maintain the pressure because of Dalton's law of partial pressures. The net loss of oxygen molecules lowers the pressure because the carbon dioxide molecules that replace them are more soluble in water and we see that result on the manometer.

■A 1.4 Leafy Reactions.

None of these three tests produced a color change. Test A, using Fehling's solution, would have indicated the presence of simple sugars with a bluish color. Test B, using Benedict's solution, would have indicated the presence of dextrose. If dextrose were present, then the mixture would have shown a rusty red color.

Even though photosynthesis produces glucose, neither of these tests shows the presence of sugar. In green leaves, the glucose produced is almost immediately stored in the leaf as starch. When we use Lugol's solution the presence of starch is indicated by the leaves turning purplish black. But the result of this test, too, was negative—no color indication. There was no starch.

Since the leaves were covered with an opaque black cloth for several days after being exposed to sunshine, the starch that had been stored was all used to sustain the plant's life processes—that is, cellular respiration. In this process, starch plus oxygen react to produce carbon dioxide and water, the reverse of photosynthesis.

For Further Reading, Research, or Study

Aldridge, B., Crow, L., and Aiuto, R. *Energy Sources and Natural Fuels,* vol. 1. Arlington, Va.: National Science Teachers Association, 1993.

This nicely illustrated book is aimed at the middle level to lower high school student. It provides a qualitative introduction to work, energy, and especially photosynthesis processes. The book uses a historical approach for photosynthesis, and it contains numerous experiments using simple materials for the student to perform. The treatment is nonquantitative and ends with research completed on photosynthesis at about 1900. The modern biochemical treatment is left to volume 2, to be published by NSTA in 1994.

Vedenov, A., and Ivanov, O. "A Burst of Green." *Quantum: The Student Magazine of Math and Science,* vol. 3, no. 5 (May/June 1993), pp. 10–14.

This article uses experiment and theory to find an explanation for the exponential growth of plants. It uses conservation of energy to create an equation that matches real leaf growth rates on earth quite closely. It is an interesting way in which physics, biology, and mathematics can be used to solve important problems.

CHAPTER 2

A FAMILY OF GENES

GENETICS is one of the hottest research areas in today's science. Such research indicates that increasingly more diseases can be associated with a genetic cause. How does this work? Does your environment have any effect on your chances of developing a particular disease? Or is it genetic? The items of this chapter focus on aspects of this exciting area of science.

■Q 2.1 How Fertile Are Sewer Rats?

Over the past 1,000 years, rats have been responsible for more loss of human life than all of the wars and revolutions combined. Rats carry not only the plague, but some twenty other deadly diseases, including cholera and typhoid fever. Consider the common sewer rat (the Norway rat, also called the brown rat) (Figure 2-1).

The gestation period for a sewer rat is about 3 weeks. Some 3 weeks after giving birth, during which time she nurtures her young, she may breed again. This means that a new litter can be produced by a female rat about every 6 weeks. The litter size is 6 to 12, with an average of about 6 *surviving* rats per litter.

When a female sewer rat is 12 weeks old, it can and will breed. Assuming that half of each litter contains females, that the typical female rat produces a new litter every 6

Figure 2-1

weeks, and all of the rats live at least 1 year, how many sewer rats can be produced in 1 year by a single pair of 12-week-old rats that breed for the first time on the first day of that year? Show how you arrive at your answer.

What is the mean age of the rat population at the end of the first year and what is the median age?

■Q 2.2 Gender Genes.

The population of a certain nation has more boys than girls. Economic and cultural pressures in this nation strongly encourage, through special privileges, that couples have only one child.

Several "official" hypotheses have been offered to account for this discrepancy between the number of boys and number of girls. One of those hypotheses is as follows: Most couples whose first child is a boy have no more children. But couples whose first child is a girl have a second child, trying again for a boy. Half of the time this second child is a boy; thus couples stop having children when the last child born is a boy. This, we are told, is why there are more boys than girls.

Does this hypothesis account for the observed surplus of boys in that nation? If not, can you offer any other hypotheses which might account for the surplus of boys?

■Q 2.3 Bacteria Genes.

Two hypotheses have been put forth concerning the origin of resistance of bacteria to antibiotics: (a) resistance is "induced" in bacteria by the presence of the antibiotic; that is, resistance is a sort of adaptation; (b) resistance is the result of a preexisting mutation that is "selected for" by the presence of the antibiotic.

Two physicists, Luria and Delbruck, attempted to distinguish between these two hypotheses using the phenomena of bacterial virus sensitivity and virus resistance. By starting with identical cultures of bacteria that are virus-sensitive, and adding identical amounts of virus at time zero, one should obtain widely different results for the recovery of virus-resistant bacteria after a given number of generations for each of these two hypotheses.

Discuss this experimental design and what the results would contribute to the resolution of the two hypotheses.

■Q 2.4 Family Genes.

The normal chromosome number in humans is 46, often written as "2n = 46," in order to indicate that chromosomes come in pairs. To be accurate, human females have 22 pairs of nonsex chromosomes (autosomes) and two X chromosomes. Human males have 22 pairs of autosomes, one X chromosome, and one Y chromosome.

Two sex chromosome abnormalities in humans are Klinefelter's syndrome, in which there is an extra chromosome — XXY— and Turner's syndrome, in which there is a missing chromosome — XO — (note that the "O" in the Turner's syndrome notation refers to a missing chromosome; also, XO is female even though there is a single X chromosome, but even though the XO has genitals, she does not generally develop secondary sex characteristics). Both are caused by the failure of sex chromosomes to separate properly during sperm or egg formation (called nondisjunction).

Using the recessive X-linked genes that cause defective color vision and hemophilia as "markers," describe an example of a family pedigree that would prove that the failure of the chromosomes to separate took place in sperm formation in the male parent.

ANSWERS FOR CHAPTER 2

◼A 2.1 How Fertile Are Sewer Rats?

You start with two rats, one male and the other female. Suppose that this pair of rats breeds for the first time on the first day of the year. The easiest way to solve this problem is to set the dates in weeks. Using the 3-week gestation time, 3-week nurture time, and 12-week maturation time, you can count children, grandchildren, great-grandchildren, and great-great-grandchildren. When done carefully, this should result in a total of 1,674 rats produced by the two original rats, for a total at the end of the year of 1,676 (Figure 2-2).

Week	Children	Grand-children from 1st litter	Grand-children from 2nd litter	Grand-children from 3rd litter	Grand-children from 4th litter	Grand-children from 5th litter	Grand-children from 6th litter	Great Grand-children from 1st litter 1st set	Great Grand-children from 1st litter 2nd set	Great Grand-children from 2nd litter 1st set
0										
3	6 (1st litter)									
6										
9	6 (2nd litter)									
12										
15	6 (3rd litter)									
18		18 (1st set)								
21	6 (4th litter)									
24		18 (2nd set)	18 (1st set)							
27	6 (5th litter)									
30		18 (3rd set)	18 (2nd set)	18 (1st set)						
33	6 (6th litter)							54		
36		18 (4th set)	18 (3rd set)	18 (2nd set)	18 (1st set)					
39	6 (7th litter)							54	54	54
42		18 (5th set)	18 (4th set)	18 (3rd set)	18 (2nd set)	18 (1st set)				
45	6 (8th litter)							54	54	54
48		8 (6th set)	18 (5th set)	18 (4th set)	18 (3rd set)	18 (2nd set)	18 (1st set)			
51	6 (9th litter)							54	54	54
54										

2 adults + 54 children + 378 grandchildren
+ 1,080 great-grandchildren
+ 162 great-great-grandchildren = 1,676 rats

Figure 2-2

Great Grand-children from ... litter set	Great Grand-children from 2nd litter 2nd set	Great Grand-children from 3rd litter 1st set	Great Grand-children from 1st litter 4th set	Great Grand-children from 2nd litter 3rd set	Great Grand-children from 3rd litter 2nd set	Great Grand-children from 4th litter 1st set	Great-great-grand children from 1st litter, 1st set, 1st 54 great-grand-children	Number of rats produced in week	Age of rats at end of year, weeks	Total number of rats at the end of each week	Week
								(2)	64	2	0
								6	49	8	3
											6
								6	43	14	9
											12
								6	37	20	15
								18	34	38	18
								6	31	44	21
								36	28	80	24
								6	25	86	27
								54	22	140	30
								60	19	200	33
								72	16	272	36
								168	13	440	39
								90	10	530	42
54	54							330	7	860	45
							162	270	4	1,130	48
54	54	54	54	54	54			546	1	1,676	51
											54

Median age = 7 weeks

Mean age $= \dfrac{\Sigma \text{ ages}}{\# \text{ rats}} = \dfrac{13{,}358}{1{,}676} = 7.97$ weeks

35

The median age of the rats is 7 weeks, and their mean age is 7.97 weeks. The median age is found by counting from the beginning of the year the number of total rats until you reach the number which is half of the final total, or until you reach 838. That time, in this case 7 weeks, is called the median age. The mean is found by forming the sum of the ages of all of the rats and dividing by the total number of rats.

You can see how the exponential growth of populations can give huge increases in short times. Also, you can see why we often say that 90% of the scientists who ever lived are alive today. You can say that about almost any occupation, when you are looking at an exponential growth situation.

By the way, from the 2 original rats, there are in 1 year 54 children, 378 grandchildren, 1,080 great-grandchildren, and 162 great-great-grandchildren.

■A 2.2 Gender Genes.

Let's simplify the problem somewhat. Suppose that we select a sample of 1,000 child-bearing couples. Then for the first child, we know from genetics that there will be 500 boys and 500 girls. Suppose that the couples who have boys have no more children. But those 500 couples who had girls have a second child. Thus this latter set of 500 couples would have, according to genetics, 250 boys and 250 girls.

Suppose that they all stop having children. How many boys and how many girls do they have? There are 750 boys and 750 girls. (For only 1,000 couples these numbers probably will not be exact, but when they are extended to millions of couples, the percentages become precisely 50% boys and 50% girls.)

Thus, the hypothesis that this can somehow account for a surplus of boys must be rejected. What other hypotheses can we offer? Sadly, the only possible hypotheses which remain are that either female fetuses are intentionally aborted or female births are unreported, with the possibility that there is even female infanticide, a tragic situation if, in fact, it exists.

◼A 2.3 Bacteria Genes.

It doesn't matter whether the characteristic is resistance to a virus (called a bacteriophage or, more simply, a phage) or to an antibiotic. Suppose that we start with separate cultures (say, ten) of virus-sensitive bacteria, each derived from a single bacterium; allow them to grow for many generations; and then expose all ten of the cultures to the virus at precisely the same time. Next we place the bacteria on solidified culture medium. The results can be of two types:

1. All ten cultures could show about the same number of virus-resistant bacterial colonies. This is consistent with the idea that the introduction of the virus "induces" the culture to adapt to the presence of the virus, since one assumes that adaptation rates after exposure are relatively constant.

2. The ten cultures could show widely fluctuating numbers of resistant colonies, since the mutation from virus-sensitive to virus-resistant could happen randomly and bacterial cells deriving from the mutation would reflect how early in the life of the culture the mutation took place.

3. A final proof would be to place a single, long-growing culture on ten separate plates, where the number of resistant colonies on each plate would be approximately the same, since all would be derived from a single event in the "mega-culture."

Luria and Delbruck obtained widely fluctuating colonies (option "b"), confirmed by "c." Thus, they demonstrated that the agent (virus or antibiotic) selects for a pre-existing mutation, and the agent does not cause the mutation. Resistance to the antibiotic is therefore not caused by some sort of adaptation.

■A 2.4 Family Genes.

Since there is no partner chromosome in the male, as there is in the XX normal female, those genes carried on the X chromosome of males are immediately expressed, even if they are recessive. Therefore, since defective color vision and hemophilia are separate, recessive, X-linked genes, they would only be expressed in females if they were present in duplicate (a very rare occurrence) or in a Turner's syndrome female. However, the recessive genes are expressed in males if they are present at all, since they cannot be hidden by additional dominant, normal genes on a partner X chromosome, as with females.

If a Turner's syndrome offspring had normal color vision and normal clotting time, and the father had both defective color vision and hemophilia, then that would indicate that non-disjunction took place in the father (i.e., the sex chromosomes failed to separate properly during sperm formation). The following illustrates this:

$X^{C,H}Y$ = male with normal color vision and normal clotting time

$X^{c,H}Y$ = male with defective color vision, normal clotting time

$X^{C,h}Y$ = male with normal color vision, hemophilia

$X^{c,h}Y$ = male with both defective color vision and hemophilia

$X^{C,H}X^{C,H}$ = normal female

$X^{C,H}X^{c,h}$ = normal female

$X^{c,H}X^{C,h}$ = normal female

Since females that have the customary number of X chromosomes are rarely color blind or hemophilic, those examples are not given.

A mother with chromosomes $X^{C,H}X^{C,H}$ crossed with a father having $X^{c,h}Y$ accounts for the following: eggs: $X^{C,H}$; sperm: $X^{c,h}Y$ or 0 (sperm with neither X nor Y).

A Turner's syndrome daughter results from the fertilization of a normal egg by an 0 sperm, and is: $X^{C,H}0$.

Since a Turner's syndrome offspring with normal color vision and normal clotting time from such a marriage could only result from the union of a normal egg with a 0 sperm, nondisjunction for such a result could only come from the male.

For Further Reading, Research or Study.

Diamond, J. "The Return of Cholera," *Discover,* vol. 13, no. 2 (February 1992).

In 1993 there were some 4,000 cases of cholera reported in Mexico. This article describes, in vivid and horrible detail, the return of this disease we all thought was from the Dark Ages. Thus, concern for rat populations is not an idle matter. And the various matters of populations and genetics are of vital concern to all of us.

Caldwell, M. "Vigil for a Doomed Virus," *Discover,* vol. 13, no. 3 (March 1992), pp. 50–57.

This is a description of the process of execution of an entire species, the virus which causes smallpox. The article offers the reader an interesting perspective on life-forms and on the challenging questions that must be answered in regard to genetics over the next several years.

CHAPTER 3

SCALING UP AND SCALING DOWN

HAVE YOU EVER watched those frightening movies that have a giant monster? Often these movies will show some ordinary animal or insect that has suddenly grown into a giant. Or have you ever tried to draw an object to scale or make something that is scaled up or down from its normal size? It is more difficult than you think. The items of this chapter address the consequences of such scaling.

3.1 A Scary Scaled-up Ant?

Movies are often based upon monsters created by some mutation induced by some chemical or radiation. The creatures are usually scaled-up versions of ants, flies, apes, or even people. Such giant monsters are shown to be scaled up proportionately. The movie *King Kong* was about such a creature—a giant ape. The giant ape might be 10 times longer, 10 times wider, and 10 times higher (Figure 3-1).

Thus it would have all of the same relative proportions as a regular size ape. But is this possible? Suppose that an ant 4 millimeters (mm) long, 2 mm high, and 2 mm wide is scaled up by some means to create a giant ant 4 meters (m) long, 2 m high and 2 m wide, an increase of all linear dimensions by a factor of 1,000 (Figure 3-2).

Figure 3-1

Figure 3-2

How much more will this ant weigh? To support this additional weight, how much stronger will its legs need to be?

■◖ 3.2 Boxed-in Spheres.

Suppose that you have a cubic box and a metal sphere that just fits inside the box. The diameter of the sphere is the same as a length of the box (Figure 3-3a).

We next fill the box with water, filling up all of the space around the metal sphere. We pour this water out and measure its volume (Figure 3-3b).

This way we know how much empty space there was in the box containing the metal sphere. Now suppose that we find eight smaller metal spheres which can just fit inside the box, so that their diameters must each be half a length of the box (Figure 3-3c).

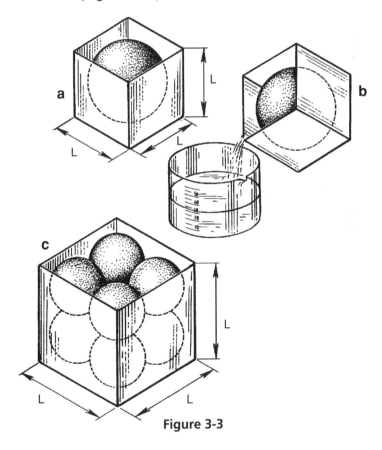

Figure 3-3

In other words, the sum of two diameters is equal to the side length. Again we pour water into the box to see how much empty space there is. Imagine continuing this process until we have a million (10^6) tiny metal spheres along one edge, a million (10^6) along the other edge, and a million (10^6) in height, with a total of a million trillion (10^{18})small metal spheres in the box. Each sphere would have a diameter of 1/1,000,000 of the side length of the box. Again we pour in water to fill the box, and pour it out to see how much empty space there was.

How does the empty space change as the metal spheres become smaller? Does that space get larger, get smaller, or stay the same? If you can do so, create an equation which gives the value of that empty space as a fraction of the total space in the box.

■◗ 3.3 Scaling Notes.

A guitar has steel strings. It is tuned to a diatonic scale, with frequencies of 165 hertz (Hz) (EE), 220 Hz (AA), 297 Hz (D), 396 Hz (G), 495 Hz (B), and 660 Hz (E). You decide you want to replace these strings with nylon strings of the same length, keeping the guitar tuned to these frequencies.

How much must the tension of the nylon strings be increased (or decreased) in comparison with the steel strings if the mass of each nylon string is one-fourth that of the corresponding steel string?

How much must the nylon string tension be increased (or decreased) compared with the steel strings if the new strings are each to be one octave higher?

■◗ 3.4 Scaling Electrical.

A 12-volt (V) lead-acid battery is 12 centimeters (cm) long, 8 cm wide, and 10 cm high. The battery is connected to an electromagnet which holds a certain iron weight up off the ground for 40 minutes (Figure 3-4).

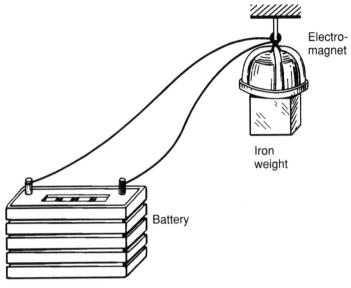

Figure 3-4

At that time, the battery has discharged so much that it can no longer hold up the iron weight, and it falls to the ground.

Another 12-volt battery, made with the same materials, but made so that every part is three times bigger in every dimension, is connected to the electromagnet. This electromagnet holds up the same iron weight. For what length of time will this 12-volt battery, 36 cm long, 24 cm wide, and 30 cm high, provide enough current to the electromagnet to hold up the iron weight?

You may assume that the internal resistances of the two batteries are the same. Explain how you arrive at your result.

■◗ 3.5 Flatland.

A map of England is scaled 1:1,000,000. Thus each distance on the map is 1,000,000 times smaller than the actual distance in England. On this map the city of London is approximately a circle with an area of about 5 square centimeters (cm²). Since there are about 7,000,000 people in London, and the map is scaled 1:1,000,000, why can't 7,000,000/1,000,000 = 7 people fit on the 5 cm² circular area of the map where London is scaled 1:1,000,000?

ANSWERS FOR CHAPTER 3

■A 3.1 A Scary Scaled-up Ant.

A giant ant, whose linear dimensions were increased by a factor of 1,000, would have its volume, and therefore its mass and weight, increased by a factor of 1 billion. It would have 1 billion times more mass than the regular size ant.

The strength of its legs, which depend upon their cross-sectional area, would be increased by $1,000^2$, or only 1 million. Thus its ratio of weight to strength would go up by a factor of 1,000. It would be like placing 1,000 ants on top of an ant and expecting the legs of the ant on the bottom to support this enormous weight. The giant creature's legs would be crushed under its own weight—hardly something to fear.

One of the most fundamental principles of natural law is that scaling up or down changes volume and areas in ways that change essential characteristics of the object being scaled. For example, heat flow in and out of objects, including organisms, is proportional to surface area, which is proportional to the square of the scaling factor. Volume of organisms, in which the metabolism of living material produces heat, goes up with the cube of that scaling factor. These two physical facts create both the upper and lower limits for the size of warm-blooded creatures.

If one argues that it is the cell size, and not the number of cells in the organism that increases as it is scaled up, there is still the same problem. When a cell is scaled up, its ability to function is also determined by the ratio of surface to volume. A cell increased by 1,000 in every linear dimension would have a mass inside that is a billion times greater, but a surface area through which oxygen, carbon dioxide, and nutrients must pass and heat be released that is only 1 million times greater. Thus it would starve and overheat.

As shown in this particular problem, the strength goes up with the square of the scaling factor and the weight goes up with the cube. This means that scaling up or down must necessarily change the appearance. Surface to volume ratios are fundamental to understanding much of living and nonliving phenomena in science.

Items like this one test such understandings.

▄A 3.2 Boxed-in Spheres.

This item could be investigated experimentally or proved mathematically. An empirical investigation would require metal spheres of at least three different sizes, set to match the box selected. You would need to get 1 sphere in the box, 8 smaller spheres in the same box, and then 27 even smaller spheres in the same box. In each case you would fill the box with water, pour it off, and see how much empty space was in the box with the spheres.

You would find that the empty space is the same in all three cases.

What is interesting about this experiment is that it *corroborates* the hypothesis that the empty space is the same, but it does not *prove* it. Since you cannot possibly test every size sphere, you must find some other way to prove that this hypothesis cannot be rejected. This can be done by using mathematical reasoning.

The volume of a box is the cube of the side length. The volume of a sphere is 4/3 times π times the cube of the radius of the sphere, which in the first case is L/2. Cubing L/2, we get 1/8 of the cube of L. Subtracting the volume of the sphere from the volume of the box we get $L^3-(4/3)\pi(1/8)L^3$, or $L^3(1-\pi/6)$. You can see that the empty space, as a fraction of total space, is just this result divided by L^3, or $1-\pi/6$. Thus for a single sphere, the fraction of empty space is $1-.5236$, or about 47.64%.

This result does not prove that this answer is correct for other size spheres. To prove it for other sizes, use some sphere of arbitrary diameter. Consider a sphere of radius r, for which N of these spheres would be along each dimension, for N^3 total spheres. For this situation, $N(2r)=L$, so that $r=L/2N$.

Then to get the fraction we would divide $L^3-N^3(4/3)\pi$ $(1/8N^3)L^3$ by the box volume L^3. We get $1-\pi/6$.

Thus the fraction of empty space is $1-\pi/6$ for *spheres of any size* which will fit into the box in the way described.

■A 3.3 Scaling Notes.

For a fixed length, the frequency of vibration of a guitar string in its fundamental mode is proportional to the square root of the tension and inversely proportional to the square root of the mass per unit of length of the string. Stated as an equation, this would be

$$f=(k/L)\sqrt{[T/(m/L)]}.$$

In this situation, if we are to keep the frequency the same, the tension must be decreased by the same factor as the mass per unit length is decreased. The lengths of the corresponding strings are the same. Thus if the string is to have its mass decreased by one-quarter, the tension of the nylon string must be decreased by the same factor. Then the guitar will retain the same frequencies.

If the nylon strings are each to be an octave higher, then instead of decreasing the tension by one-quarter, we must keep the tension of the nylon the same as it was for steel strings.

48

■A 3.4 Scaling Electrical.

A battery has plates that interact with an electrolyte (Figure 3-5). This chemical reaction is determined by the surface areas of the battery plates. If you double the surface area of the battery plates, you will double the total number of electric charges that the battery can send through some given external circuit. The voltage of the battery, which provides the push, is determined entirely by the materials of which the plates and electrolyte are made (assuming that the batteries have the same number of cells).

Since volume, and therefore mass, goes up with the cube of the scaling factor, one might expect the available substance in the battery to provide 27 times more additional charges. But this does not happen.

In a lead storage battery, both electrodes are lead. When fully charged, one lead electrode has a layer of lead dioxide, while the other is pure lead. The electrolyte is sulfuric acid. When fully discharged, the lead dioxide layer is gone from one electrode, and both electrodes have a layer of lead sulfate. These layers have the same thickness, regardless of battery size. Thus, the availability of charges is a surface effect, not a volume effect.

Increasing the dimensions of the battery by a factor of 3 means that the battery will have three squared (3^2),

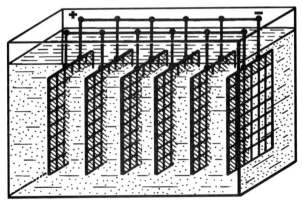

Figure 3-5

or 9 times more surface area, and three cubed (3^3), or 27 times, more volume (and therefore 27 times more mass). The battery will therefore be able to push a total of 9 times more electric charges through an external circuit before running down. This larger battery will keep the electromagnet sufficiently strong to hold the iron weight for 9 times 40 minutes, or 360 minutes, or 6 hours.

You can see why a small 9-volt battery cannot provide as much energy as a much larger 3-volt or 6-volt battery. This problem is an example of another kind of scaling-law problem. There are many such situations in science.

◢A 3.5 Flatland.

The map is scaled 1:1,000,000. This means that the linear scaling factor is 1/1,000,000. This item illustrates a common preconception error associated with scaling—using a linear scaling factor for a variable associated with an area. A map gives an area, and the area goes with the square of the scaling factor. Thus, in terms of area, the map is $(1/1,000,000)^2 = 1/1,000,000,000,000$ as big as the country.

In the case of London, for example, we could get only (7,000,000) x (1/1,000,000,000,000) people onto the map of London. This would be 7/1,000,000 of one person. People are not packed, standing next to each other, in London. This is why we get such a small fraction of one person even for the 5 square centimeters (5 cm^2) of map surface.

For Further Reading, Research, or Study

Haldane, J. "On Being the Right Size," *The World of Mathematics,* vol. 2 (New York: Simon and Schuster, 1956), pp. 950–57.

Abbott, E. "Flatland", *The World of Mathematics,* vol. 4, (New York: Simon and Schuster) pp. 2385–96.

The first of these two short pieces concerns scaling of living systems. The second looks at a world of two dimensions, instead of three.

The first piece is a brief but powerful analysis of the scaling effects on living creatures on earth. It will give the reader a vastly different perspective on scaling up and down and will reveal the very real limitations of geometry on biology.

The second piece puts you in a world of two dimensions and forces you to imagine a world in which you do not live—one of three dimensions. This is an important exercise, since much of our understanding of modern mathematics and physics requires that we work in spaces having more than 3 dimensions. It provides a uniquely different view of scaling.

CHAPTER 4

HOW FAST IS FAST?

IT SEEMS sometimes that speed is everything, and we all want to go as fast as we can in everything we do. The items that follow will focus on the fact that how we compute average speeds is not always simple and on the fact that the velocity of an object depends upon your point of view.

4.1 Check Your Speed.

You are driving a car along a long straight part of an interstate highway. You drive 10 miles at precisely 60 miles per hour (mph), when you come to some highway construction. You then slow immediately to 30 mph and drive at precisely 30 mph for the next 10 miles. What was your average speed over that 20 miles of interstate highway?

Show how you arrived at your answer.

4.2 Bridging the Gap.

You are driving on a bridge that is 2 miles long. You manage to drive the first mile in 2 minutes. How fast must you drive the rest of the way to cross the bridge with an average speed of 60 mph?

4.3 Where's My Apple?

You are riding in a car with your window open. The car is traveling at 30 mph along a straight, flat road. You drop

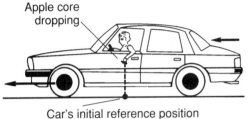

Apple core
dropping

Car's initial reference position

Figure 4-1

(but do not throw) an apple core out the window (and it is quickly gobbled up by hungry birds). For this item we assume that air resistance is negligible (Figure 4-1).

In terms of where the car *was* when you let go of the apple core, where does the core hit the ground? Where the car *was*? Behind where the car *was*? Or in front of where the car *was*? In terms of where the car *is* at the instant the core hits the ground, where does the core hit? Where the car *is*? Behind where the car *is*? Or in front of where the car *is*? As a reference point, use the position of the car as some point on the car's body directly below where the apple core was released.

Explain how you arrive at your answers. If necessary, use sketches to show the apple core and car.

■◗ 4.4 Trains are for the Birds.

Two trains are speeding toward one another on the same track at 40 mph. When they are 8 miles apart, a bird leaves the front of one train and flies at 60 mph toward the other train. When it reaches that train, the bird turns around and flies back toward the other oncoming train, turning around again when it reaches the train (Figure 4-2).

The bird continues this back-and-forth flight until the two trains collide, just after the bird moves aside enough not to get caught. How far did the bird fly in its back-and-forth motion?

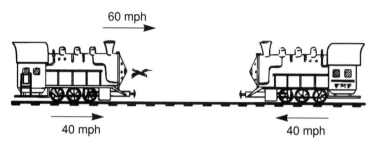

60 mph

40 mph   40 mph

Figure 4-2

ANSWERS FOR CHAPTER 4

■**A** 4.1 Check your Speed.

This item is most often calculated incorrectly because of a preconception most people have about the concept of average. To them an average is found by taking two or more numbers, adding them, and dividing the sum by the number of numbers that were added. But even though this method could be used in this case, it could be correct only by using various speeds for every instant of time (Figure 4-3).

The concept of average speed is very specific. It requires that you find the total distance and divide it by the time it takes to travel that distance. In this problem, the first 10 miles is traveled at 60 mph, or 1 mile per minute. Thus it takes 10 minutes to travel 10 miles. The next 10 miles is traveled at half that speed, or 30 mph. It must take 2 minutes for every mile for that 10 miles. Thus for the last 10 miles, it required 20 minutes.

The total time traveled was therefore 30 minutes or 1 half hour. Traveling 20 miles in 1/2 hour means that your average speed was 40 mph. Note that this is not the same result as taking 60 mph plus 30 mph and dividing by 2, which would give 45 mph, an incorrect answer.

The importance of this item is the fact that average

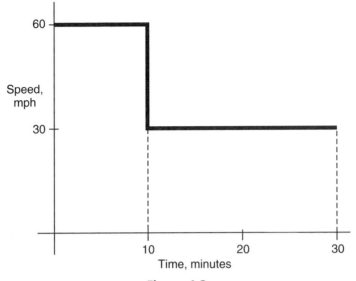

Figure 4-3

speed is a fundamental concept. Without an understanding of such fundamental concepts, one cannot properly understand more complex phenomena or problems or issues involving quantities derived from this concept, quantities like acceleration, force, kinetic energy, power, and so forth.

◼️A 4.2 Bridging the Gap.

In the first 2 minutes you travel only halfway across the 2-mile bridge. In order to average 60 mph in crossing the 2-mile bridge, you must cross the entire bridge in 2 minutes (since 60 mph is a mile per minute). There is therefore no speed fast enough for you to average 60 mph if it took you 2 minutes to go halfway across.

◼️A 4.3 Where's My Apple?

This item tests your understanding of the concept of relative velocity. When the apple core is dropped, it contin-

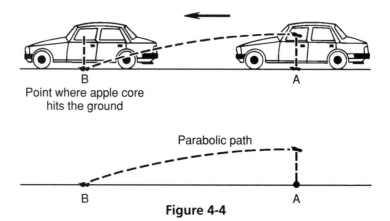

B

Point where apple core
hits the ground

A

Parabolic path

B

A

Figure 4-4

ues to move horizontally (ignoring air resistance) at the same speed as the car, 30 mph. But it accelerates downward at the rate given for that location on the earth, nearly 32 feet/second/second (ft/s/s).

The core will hit the ground ahead of where the car was when you dropped the core (Figure 4-4).

From the point of view of the moving car, the apple core falls straight downward. From the point of view of an observer standing on the ground outside the car, the apple core will follow a parabolic path, like that of a projectile fired horizontally at 30 mph.

▰A 4.4 Trains Are for the Birds.

This is one of those problems whose solution can be very hard or very easy. The trains are each moving at 40 mph, and they are moving toward each other on the same track. This means that their relative velocity is 80 mph. Since they are 8 miles apart when the bird leaves the first train heading toward the other, it will take the trains 6 minutes to collide. (They will travel for 8 mi/80 mph = 1/10 hour, or 6 minutes.)

Since the bird is flying at 60 mph, or 1 mile per minute, it will travel back and forth a total distance of 6 miles. This was the easy solution. The hard solution is to consider the infinite series that results from taking how far the bird travels in each segment and adding the distances. This forms an infinite series which also sums to 6 miles.

For Further Reading, Research, or Study

Arons, A. *A Guide to Introductory Physics Teaching,* (New York: John Wiley & Sons, 1990), pp. 20–43.

This book for physics teachers offers the student considerable insight into the kinds of problems he or she and other students have in forming concepts involving time, speed, velocity, and acceleration. The book offers a very different treatment than can be found in any physics textbook. Arons offers a wealth of experience from having worked with students over more than 50 years.

Hewitt, P. *Conceptual Physics,* 6th ed. (Boston: Scott, Foresman and Company, 1989), chaps. 2–3.

This is one of the few textbooks offered as a reference for this quiz book. Paul Hewitt learned physics late in life. He has a profound understanding of the basic concepts, and he knows how to express them in ways that students understand. This makes his text an excellent reference for gaining a feeling for a concept before having to use it in its more abstract forms.

MAKING SENSE OF IT

OUR SENSES are very important to all of us because they allow us to see, feel, hear, and smell the environment around us. Without our senses, we could not function. But senses have their limitations and interesting, unexpected benefits. We will now look at some of those.

■Q 5.1 Can You Feel It?

When a 1,200-gram (g) weight is placed on your wrist, you cannot perceive an increase in pressure until an additional 40 g is added. When 30 g is placed on your wrist you need an additional 1 g to perceive the change (Figure 5-1).

How many grams would have to be added to a weight of 600 g on your wrist to be perceptible?

What would you feel if a weight of 64 ounces (oz) on your wrist had added to it an additional weight of 1 oz? Explain how you arrived at the latter answer.

■Q 5.2 Hearing Those Ratios.

Frequency differences from notes of musical instruments are detected by humans according to frequency ratios, not differences. Also, musical intervals are always expressed as frequency ratios, not differences.

Two frequencies produced from a musical instrument

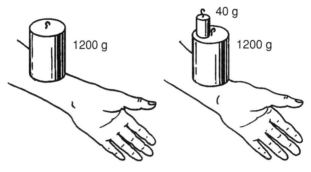

Figure 5-1

are said to differ by an octave when they are in a ratio of 2:1. A piano has 12 keys for each octave (Figure 5-2).

Suppose that you want to tune the piano so that each note has a frequency that is higher than that of the previous note by a fixed factor. This means that the frequencies of any two adjacent notes on the piano have the same ratio. What is this ratio?

If the frequency of A above middle C is 440 hertz (Hz), what are the frequencies of the three notes above

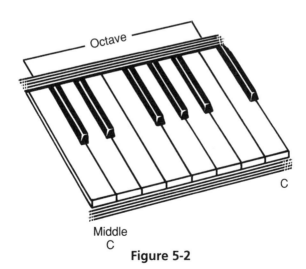

Figure 5-2

A and the nine notes below A? Such a piano is said to be tuned to an even-tempered (or equally tempered) scale.

■◗ 5.3 Seeing the Light.

Suppose that a point source of light is located in a large room without windows, with the walls painted a flat black. You do not start the following experiment until your eyes have adjusted to the darkness (so that the pupil in each eye is wide open). You can control the intensity of the light, and you have a friend adjust the light level until, at a distance of 100 feet (ft) it is just barely visible (Figure 5-3).

When your friend turns the light intensity down even slightly, it is not visible to your eye. With the light set at this barely perceptible level, you begin to move measured distances toward the light. As you move closer, you perceive that the light gets brighter.

How much brighter do you perceive the light to be when you are 25 ft from the source than when you are 50 ft from the source?

How much greater is the illumination from this light source on a certain fixed surface area placed normal to the light rays at 25 ft than at 50 ft?

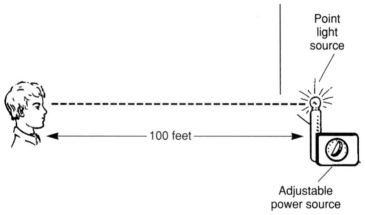

Figure 5-3

A 5.1 Can You Feel It?

In this particular problem, which involves pressure, the basic information is given. To be perceptible, 1/30 of the amount acting must be added. Thus for 600 g, 20 g must be added to be perceptible.

If 1 oz is added to 64 oz, you will not notice the additional weight because it is below the perceptible threshold of 1/30 of 64 oz, or 2.1 oz.

A 5.2 Hearing Those Ratios.

The musical interval called an octave exists whenever the frequency of the higher note is twice that of the lower note. On a piano, there are seven white keys and five black keys from middle C to C above middle C.

If we tune the piano for an even-tempered scale, the musical interval between each adjacent pair of the 12 keys in an octave must be the same. That is, the ratio of the frequency of one note to the next lower note must be the same for all pairs of keys on the piano. But we must also have the keys tuned so that the frequency of C above middle C is twice the frequency of middle C.

Let R represent the unknown ratio of frequencies from one note to the next. Then if f_C is the frequency of middle C, the first key above middle C, namely C#, must have a frequency of Rf_C. The next key above C#, namely D, must have a frequency of R times that of C#. Thus, D above middle C must have a frequency of $R(Rf_C)$, or R^2f_C. The next higher key, the black key D# must have a frequency of R times that of D. Therefore this key must have a frequency of $R(R^2f_C)$, or R^3f_C. Continuing in this way, we can keep multiplying by the ratio R until we get to C above middle C. At that key, which is an octave above middle C, we would have for the frequency $R^{12}f_C$. But we know that an octave represents a frequency ratio of exactly 2. Therefore, we must have $R^{12} = 2$.

This equation can be solved by taking the 12th root of both sides of the equation. The 12th root of R^{12} is simply R, the ratio we are trying to find. The 12th root of 2 can be found by using a hand calculator with logarithms. You can find the logarithm of 2, divide it by 12, and find the antilogarithm of that result. When you do this calculation, you find that the value of the ratio R is 1.059463094.

Since A above middle C is, by international agreement, exactly 440 Hz, the first note above A (the black key A#) must have a frequency of 440x(1.059463094), or 466.16 Hz. The next higher key (white key B) must have a frequency of 466.16 x (1.059463094), or 493.88 Hz. Finally, the frequency of C above middle C must have a frequency of 493.88x(1.059463094), or 523.25 Hz. Since middle C must have half this frequency, middle C must have a frequency of 261.63 Hz. The nine notes above middle C must have frequencies of 277.18 (C#), 293.66 (D), 311.13 (D#), 329.63 (E), 349.23 (F), 369.99 (F#), 392.00 (G), and 415.31 (G#).

It is unlikely that anyone would want a piano tuned to such frequencies, although musical pieces have been created for pianos tuned approximately to an even-tempered scale.

■A 5.3 Seeing the Light.

Items like this one are very important. Each is an example of a very general empirical law of science that transcends disciplines, especially biology, chemistry, and physics. The law is called the *Weber-Fechner law of biology.* This is an empirical law that summarizes the observation that a stimulus is detectable only if it exceeds an amount that is proportional to the stimulus already acting.

For light, the proportionality constant is about 1/120. For sound it is about 1/9, and for touch it is 1/30. There are similar ratios for other senses, like that of taste in terms of bitterness. When the relationship involves the fact that the needed stimulus must be proportional to the stimulus already acting, the behavior is logarithmic. Hence the use of decibels in sound, pH in acidity, and our method of ascertaining the magnitude of stars, which is logarithmic. This item illustrates the difference between the physical properties of light intensity and illumination and the perception of brightness by the human eye.

If you ask someone how much brighter a light source should appear as you reduce your distance to the source by one-half, the first reaction is to use the inverse square law. This law, which is correct for the illumination on a surface, would require that the illumination increase by a factor of 4 as you move to where you are half as far away from the light source. Thus, in this case, at 25 ft, the actual brightness in terms of illumination in lumens/square meter is four times greater than it was at 50 ft.

But what you perceive as brightness is not four times greater. Your eyes respond to brightness in such a way that you can detect a difference in brightness only when the new illumination is 1.0083 times that of the prior level. Your eyes respond to light logarithmically, not linearly.

As you walk halfway toward the light source, at 50 ft, the light entering your eyes is 4 times brighter. But that factor of 4 must be equal to the product of the number of factors of 1.0083 (the number of perceptible differences in intensity of light) you would be able to count as you walked that 50 ft. If you set $(1.0083)^n = 4$, and solve this equation for n, you will get 167 steps of perceptible change (from where the light was barely perceptible) to that halfway point. To solve the equation, use logarithms, in which case $n=(\log_{10} 4)/(\log_{10} 1.0083)$, or n= 168. As you continue to walk, and reach one-quarter of the total distance, at 25 ft, you counted 168 additional steps of perceptible change. From 100 ft to 25 ft, you would have counted a total of

336 perceptible differences. This is twice the number counted from 100 ft to 50 ft. Therefore, from the 50-ft point to the 25-ft point, your eye perceived the light as increasing in brightness by a factor of 2, while, according to the inverse square law, the actual physical illumination increased by a factor of 4.

As you move from 25 ft to 12.5 ft, cutting your distance again in half, the physical illumination goes up again by a factor of 4. But your perception goes up to 504 discernible steps, an increase by a factor of 1.5. From 12.5 ft to 6.25 ft provides another factor of 4 increase in illumination, but a perceptible factor of only 672/504, or 1.33.

The equation for the number of discernible steps from barely perceptible is given by

$$n = 279 \log_{10} (I_n/I_o),$$

where I_n is the illumination at step number n and I_o is the illumination when the light is barely perceptible. In terms of distances, r_n and r_o, the inverse square law for light is given by

$$I_n/I_o=(r_o/r_n)^2.$$

Using these values of illumination, the discernible step equation becomes

$$n=558 \log_{10}(r_o/r_n).$$

Thus the closer you get, and the greater the illumination, the less the eye responds.

This is a good example of the Weber-Fechner law from biology. Your senses respond logarithmically to changes in intensities, probably as a protection mechanism against wide fluctuations of light, sound, pressure, and other stimuli, all of which obey this law. This item helps you understand why, historically, the brightnesses of stars were recorded in terms of apparent magnitudes, which formed a logarithmic scale.

For Further Reading, Research, or Study

Strassenburg, A., Aldridge, B., and Waldman, G. *The Guitar: A Module on Wave Motion and Sound* (American Institute of Physics, 1975), pp. 24–46. (Available through American Association of Physics Teachers, College Park, Md.), Section B.

This monograph carefully develops the concepts associated with the physics of a guitar, how frequencies and sound intensities are heard, and wave motion as applied to a guitar. It is excellent background for students who want to understand the physics of stringed instruments.

Smith, J. *Senses and Sensibilities,* (New York: John Wiley & Sons, 1989), chap. 5.

Chapter 5 of this book examines the senses, their structure and function. It also considers the nature of sensations and their relation to sensory apparatus.

CHAPTER 6

HEAVENLY DIMENSIONS

ALL OF US have seen the moon and the sun. But do we really notice their size and direction? Directions and sizes are very important in astronomy. Sometimes our langugage confuses us. Have you ever heard someone say, "I am going downtown" or "I am going up north"? What does all of this mean? Is north really up and is the town really down?

These next few items will focus on directions and sizes of such "heavenly dimensions." You should schedule yourself for some sky gazing if you really want to be certain of some of your answers.

■Q 6.1 Lunar Directions.

You live in a midwestern town in the United States. It is 11:00 P.M. in late September, and when you look into the night sky, slightly south of west, you see the moon just above the horizon (elevated about 15°). Sketch a picture of how the moon will appear at that time.

If it is not a full moon, show which side of the moon disc facing the Earth is dark and which side is illuminated by the sun. Where will the moon be the next night at the same time? Higher or lower in the sky?

■Q 6.2 Which Way Is Up?

An operational definition is stated in terms of how to observe, measure, construct, or do something that con-

stitutes the defined quantity. Can you create an operational definition for the term *vertical*? How about *horizontal*?
These definitions should be stated in terms of some location on earth.

■Q 6.3 Moon-Size Pies.

It is evening, and you look out your window and see a full
moon. If you were to hold a small disc up at arm's length
(about 2 ft away), what diameter must it be to just eclipse
the disc of the moon? It must be just the right size so you
cannot see the moon's illuminated disc (Figure 6-1).

Ask other people the same question to see what they
think. You should also try to observe a full moon and do
this little experiment. Then carefully explain *why* you get
the result you do, and if you and others have made a wrong
estimate, explain why your estimate was wrong.

What would be the diameter of a disc held at arm's
length that would just obscure the disc of the sun (do not
look directly at the sun, as it could injure your eyes)?
Again, why do we get the result that we do, and how can
you reconcile this result with what you thought it would
be?

■Q 6.4 A Mighty Long Shadow.

When are shadows cast toward the south in Houston,
Texas? That is, when is there a component of the shadow

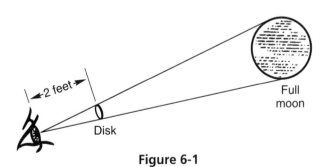

Figure 6-1

of a vertical pole that is toward the south? A teacher who asked this question told his class that since the maximum tilt of the Earth's axis with the pole of the ecliptic was 23.45° and Houston was at 29.77° north latitude, the sun could *never* cast a shadow there with a southerly component. (The *pole of the ecliptic* is an imaginary line from the sun through the North Star. Thus the ecliptic is the plane in which Earth revolves around the sun.) We would be short some 6.32°.

Is the teacher correct? If not, given the preceding correct data, how can you explain how and when a shadow could be cast toward the south in Houston?

◼**A** 6.1 Lunar Directions.

This item can be answered using two sources: using knowledge of the relative positions and motions of the Earth-sun-moon system, which is far more complicated than most people think, or recalling observations that you have made.

In the former case, one is using a model or theory to account for or predict an observation. In the latter case, one is summarizing observations, with no attempt to explain or account for what is observed.

Everyone should have had the experience some time in his or her life of keeping an Earth-moon-sun log. Making such observations daily over a period of a year provides extremely valuable insights into simple astronomy.

From such observations, if carefully made, one can create models of various kinds to account for what has been observed. Through such activities a person can come to understand how difficult it is to use evidence from observations to create even a simple model for the motions of our part of the solar system.

In this item, if the moon were in the southwestern sky just above the horizon at 11 P.M., then it must have been approximately overhead at sunset, 5 hours earlier.

If the moon is nearly overhead at sunset, then the sun must have been shining on half of what appears to be a moon disc. It would be that half of the moon's disc that is to the right, with the darker half of the moon to the left (Figure 6-2a).

As the evening passes, the moon appears to move westward across the sky, and by 11:00 P.M. it is seen in the southwestern sky, with the sun illuminating the lower right half of that disc (Figure 6-2b).

Notice that the question does not ask for the phase, the quarter, or other such terminology. Those terms

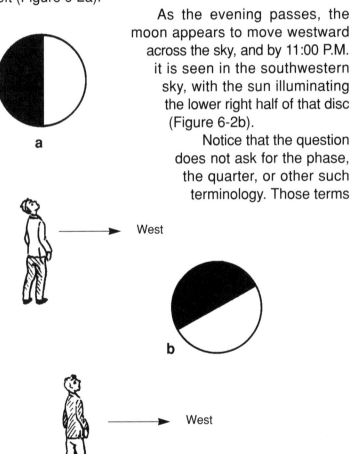

a

West

b

West

Figure 6-2

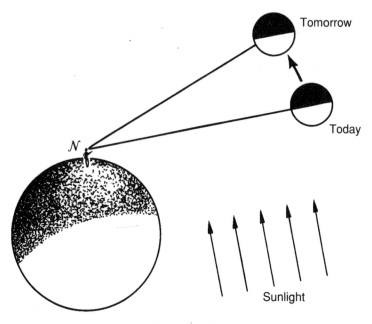

Figure 6-3

are merely names, and, without experience with observations, they mean nothing.

Where will the moon be tomorrow night at the same time? Again, from theory, one can conclude that since the moon is revolving around the earth in the same direction as the Earth's rotation, the moon should be higher in the sky (Figure 6-3).

By observation, one would recall the same result but could offer no explanation of why.

All of us have observed the moon hundreds of times. It would be surprising if you could not answer this item correctly. If you also had previously learned the relative positions and motions of the Earth-sun-moon system but could not answer the question, then you can see how memorization of facts does not help you achieve real understanding.

■A 6.2 Which Way Is Up?

We use words like *vertical* and *horizontal* without really thinking about how we would determine what they mean. Yet a carpenter or brick mason would understand perfectly well how to determine *operationally* when something is vertical or horizontal. A line is vertical if it coincides with, or is parallel to, a plumb bob.

A plumb bob is a small weight on the end of a string. When you hold it up close to a wall or column you are building, it should be aligned with the wall in such a way that the distance from the string to the wall is constant, all the way up. With a plumb bob you can determine what is locally vertical.

A line or top of a brick wall is horizontal if a line along that wall is always at right angles to a vertical. Thus, once you have a vertical, you can just measure with a protractor. But what if you do not have a protractor? Then you must somehow make one. An easier method is to use a level. A bubble inside it shows when a level is being held horizontal. The level depends upon the fact that the local value of the gravitational force is constant over short distances. Thus if the level is not actually horizontal, the bubble will move to one side of a center position.

Bubble levels are used extensively in construction work. Both levels and plumb bobs, or their more sophisticated electronic counterparts, are used extensively in science and technology.

■A 6.3 Moon-Size Pies.

You can easily answer this question yourself through direct experience. If you took the trouble to make the observation of the full moon, you may have been surprised. The moon has a diameter of 2,160 miles and is at times as close as 226,000 miles and at other times as far away as 252,000 miles, with a mean distance of 239,000 miles from the Earth. This means that on the average the moon subtends an angle, in radians of 2,160/239,000, or about 0.0090 radian.

At its closest point (perigee) the angle is 2,160/226,000, or 0.0096 radian. At its farthest distance from the earth (*apogee*), the angle is 2,160/252,000, or 0.0086 radian. At a distance of 2 ft from your eye, a disc that would subtend that same angle would have a diameter of 2 x 0.0090 ft, or 0.018 ft. This would be 0.22 inch, or about 7/32 of an inch. In metric units this would be about 5.5 mm, or about a half of a centimeter. At perigee, the eclipsing disc would have a diameter of 5.9 mm, and at apogee, 5.3 mm.

If you are unfamiliar with the angular measurements in radians, you can also solve this problem using similar triangles. The simplest description is as shown in Figure 6.4. Since the triangle formed by your eye with a diameter of the moon is similar to the triangle formed by your eye and the disc (the two triangles have the same angles; therefore, all sides stand in the same proportion), even though we will not be using a ratio of sides of these triangles when using the average distance to the moon and the distance to the disc, those distances are corresponding linear measures for each triangle and, therefore, also stand in the same ratio when the triangles are similar (if you think this is too complicated, then create two similar triangles using radii of the moon and disc; then the distances are sides of those triangles). In any case, we must have d/2 = 2,160/239,000, or, more simply, d=0.018 ft, as before.

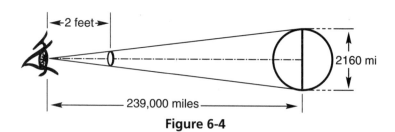

Figure 6-4

This result is much smaller than most people would estimate from their experience. Now why is that? Mostly you see the moon's disc next to other objects that are nearby on the Earth. For example, you might see the full moon rising, with buildings or trees in the same scene. You tend to judge the size of the moon by the sizes of these other objects whose sizes you know. For example, a house 20 ft high 2,220 ft away would subtend the same angle as the moon. It would look about the same height. If you saw the moon's disc next to such a house at that distance, it would be natural to misjudge the moon's great distance. That would tend to make you believe that the angle subtended by the moon is larger than it really is.

The disc of the sun subtends almost the same angle on Earth as does that of the moon. The sun is, on the average, 92,900,000 miles from the earth, and the sun has a diameter of 864,100 miles. Thus, the sun's disc subtends an angle of 864,100/92,900,000, or 0.0093 radian. The size of a disc at 2 ft needed to eclipse the sun is just slightly larger than needed to eclipse the moon, about 5.7 mm.

Of course the sun is also closest to the earth in January when the angle is 864,100/91,500,000, or 0.0094, for a disc size of about 5.7 mm at 2 ft. In July, when the sun is at its greatest distance away, the angle is 0.0091, for a disc size of about 5.5 mm. This result, too, is probably much smaller than you expected. The reason you thought it should be larger is the same as for the moon. Interestingly, the size of the disc to eclipse the moon is between 5.3 mm and 5.9 mm, while the size to eclipse the sun is between 5.5 mm and 5.7 mm. You can see that for all practical purposes, the apparent sizes of the moon and sun are the same.

■A 6.4 A Mighty Long Shadow.

The teacher is partially correct. There can never be a shadow cast toward the south in Houston when the sun is at its maximum inclination (at astronomical noon). But in the morning and afternoon, there are times when shadows are most assuredly cast toward the south.

The simplest situation to consider is at sunrise. Consider June 21, when the sun appears to be at its northernmost position. At noon there can be no shadow toward the south. But at sunrise the angle between the sun's rays and the shadow cast by a vertical pole is no longer determined entirely by the Earth's angle of tilt. The latitude is an important factor.

Taking the latitude into account, there is a shadow cast toward the south at sunrise and sunset for locations in the Northern Hemisphere between March 20 and September 23, with maximum shadows toward the south at sunrise on June 21. The shadows are toward the south from sunrise to about 9:00 A.M. and again between 3 P.M. and sunset. At sunrise and sunset on these days in Houston, the shadow cast by the sun's rays makes an angle of about 26° south of an east-west line.

Although the mathematical proof of this fact is complex, you can illustrate this by means of a model, consisting of a ball, or preferably a globe, with a vertical pin placed at your own location, or at some other latitude and longitude. Then the ball (or globe) can be rotated with its axis at some angle with respect to the sun (or a narrow-beam floodlight placed some distance away). You will see how the shadow is affected by different amounts of rotation and at different orientations with respect to the sun.

The simplest mathematical proof requires that you treat the earth as a sphere. Then you must find unit vectors for up and north. By forming a cross-product of up and north, you get a unit vector for west. Using these three vectors, along with the vector that specifies the direction of the sun's rays, you can find components of shadows at any time of the day or year. The same thing can be done treating the Earth as an oblate spheroid, but the math becomes more complicated, requiring the use of calculus. The results for an oblate spheroid are not greatly different from those for a sphere.

For Further Reading, Research, or Study

Schaaf, F. *Seeing the Sky: 100 Projects, Activities, and Explorations in Astronomy* (New York: John Wiley & Sons, 1990), chap. 6.

This book offers the student ideas for astronomy projects. It emphasizes observation, and the many good illustrations help the reader better understand astronomy.

Gardner, R. *Famous Experiments You Can Do.* (New York: Franklin Watts, 1990). pp. 24–33.

This excellent little book offers numerous, well-illustrated and simple experiments in science. Most of these are classical experiments performed by great scientists. They are described so that they can be carried out with simple apparatus.

CHAPTER 7

EUREKA!

■Q 7.1 Playing with Density.

Suppose that you weigh a glass full of water. Then suppose that you weigh an identical glass that is full of water but has a wooden block, partially submerged, and partially out of the water, but floating in it (Figure 7-1). Which would weigh more? Explain your answer.

■Q 7.2 Sink or Swim.

A large tank is filled with water. Salt is dissolved in the tank of water until a person of mass 80 kilograms (kg) can just float freely in the tank. In other words, the person, holding her breath with a normal amount of air in her lungs,

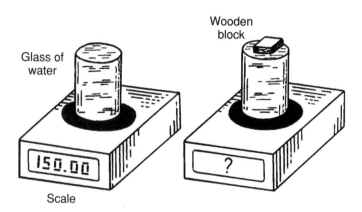

Figure 7-1

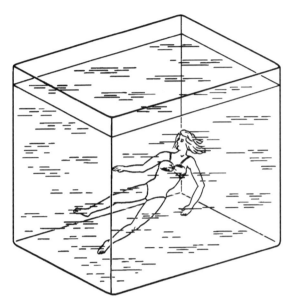

Figure 7-2

does not sink to the bottom of the tank or rise to the top. She is submerged, but suspended (Figure 7-2).

A 100 milliliter (ml) sample of the salt water has a mass of 105 grams (g). Using this information, what is the volume of this person's body? Show how you arrive at your answer.

◼◗ 7.3 How Heavy Is the Cargo?

A toy boat carries a block of iron having a mass of 200 g. It floats in a pan of water, on which a 200 g block of wood is also floating, with 20% of its volume above the water's surface (Figure 7-3).

Suppose that the iron block is removed from the boat, then allowed to sink to the bottom of the pan of water, and the wooden block is lifted from the water and placed in the toy boat. How does the water level in the pan compare with what it was when the boat carried the iron block?

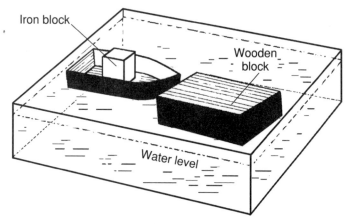

Figure 7-3

■Q 7.4 Genuine Gold Ring for Sale?

A friend wants to sell you a gold ring for $100. He says that the ring is 22 carat gold. You decide to investigate his claim before buying the ring at that price.

Gold jewelry is usually made of alloys of gold (density of 19.3 grams/cubic centimeter [g/cm³]), silver (density of 10.5 g/cm³), copper (density of 8.96 g/cm³), and sometimes platinum. Gold-colored jewelry is an alloy of gold, silver, and copper, with the copper being used to give the gold a reddish tinge. Silver and gold alloy produces "white gold." This particular ring has a gold colored appearance; therefore it must have in it gold, copper, and possibly some silver.

Suppose that the ring has a mass of 9.20 g when weighed in air. When it is suspended in water, its mass reading is 8.70 g (Figure 7-4).

From these measurements, what is the volume of the ring? What is its density? Approximately what carat ring is it (24 carats is 100% gold). How much per ounce is your friend asking you to pay for the gold that is in the ring?

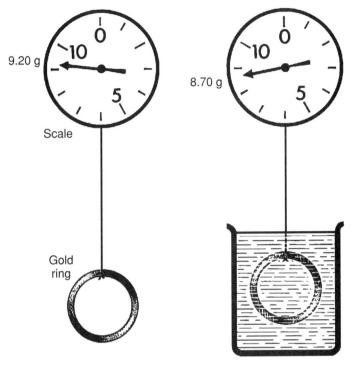

Figure 7-4

▰**A 7.1 Playing with Density.**

This item tests your understanding of Archimedes' principle. In the first case the glass is full of water and has a certain weight. When a wooden block is placed into an identical glass full of water, the block displaces an amount of water equal to the block's weight. Thus, this volume of water, having a weight equal to the block's weight, over-flows and is no longer in the glass.

But the total weight of the glass, water, and block is the same as before the block was placed in the glass. Thus the two glasses of water, one with and the other without the block, weigh the same.

▪A 7.2 Sink or Swim.

This item is a variation of a common method of determining percentage of fat in one's body, as done in physical fitness centers. There are tables of densities and other variables that enable you to determine your fat content versus other kinds of tissue.

In this item, if one is suspended in the salt water, then one's average density is the same as the average density of the water. Of course, this density would change according to how much air you have in your lungs and how much fat is in your body.

In this case the density of the person must be 1.05 g/ml. With a mass of 80 kg, or 80,000 g, there must be 1 ml volume for every 1/1.05 g, or 0.952 cm³/g. Thus the person's volume must be 80,000 g multiplied by .952 cm³/g, giving the result 76,160 cm³, or 76.16 liters (l).

▪A 7.3 How Heavy Is the Cargo?

When the iron block is in the toy boat, its weight must be supported by the boat. This means that the boat must, according to Archimedes' principle (see A7.1), displace a weight of water equal to that of the boat and its load. There must be 200 g of water displaced by the iron block while it is carried in the toy boat.

Since the wooden block is floating, and it has a mass of 200 g, it, too, must displace 200 g of water. The fact that 20% of its volume is above the surface of the water merely indicates the density of the wood. This information is otherwise irrelevant to the problem.

When the iron block is removed from the toy boat and allowed to sink to the bottom of the pan, the iron block no longer must displace a volume of water having a weight equal to the iron. Indeed, since the iron sinks to the bottom, most of the force upward is supplied by the bottom of the pan itself.

The wooden block, when placed in the toy boat, still

must produce a displacement of water with a mass equal to that of the wooden block. The net result is caused therefore by the iron block alone. It displaces less water than when it was being floated by the boat; therefore, the water level in the pan must fall.

Some readers may have difficulty following a line of reasoning which is somewhat abstract. When that happens, you will find it useful to use a more concrete example. Then it is easier to generalize to the abstract. In this case, you decide that the boat has some mass, say 400 g. Then the boat plus iron has a mass of 600 g. This combination must displace 600 g, or 600 ml, of water. The 200 g block of wood which is floating beside the boat displaces an additional 200 g of water, or 200 ml. Thus there is 800 ml of water being displaced initially by the boat, the iron block it is carrying, and the floating wooden block. Now we take the iron block out of the boat. While we hold the iron block, the water level must go down by an amount equivalent to the 200 ml of water displaced by 200 g of iron. When we place the wooden block into the boat, we have simply taken 200 g and allowed it to displace the 200 ml by means of the boat rather than by floating next to the boat. When we allow the iron block to sink to the bottom, it will displace an amount of water equal to its volume. But because the iron block is more dense than water, the mass of water displaced will be less than the mass of the iron. Thus the water level must drop.

▰A 7.4 Genuine Gold Ring for Sale?

This gold ring has a mass of 9.20 g when measured in air. When suspended in water, it has a mass reading of 8.70 g. The mass difference, according to Archimedes' principle, is equal to the mass of water displaced, or 0.50 g. Since water has a specific gravity of 1, the volume displaced is 0.50 cm^3. The ring must therefore have a density of 9.20 g/0.50 cm^3, which is 18.4 g/cm^3.

If, as claimed, the ring is 22 carat, it should have 22/24 = 91.7% gold and 8.3% other metal, probably copper. When we find the sum of (.917)(19.3 g/cm³) and (.083)(8.96 g/cm³), we have 18.4 g/cm³ for the required density. The ring certainly is 22 carat gold, and it appears to be alloyed with copper.

There are 31.1 g in 1 troy ounce (based on 12 ounces per pound [oz/lb])) and 28.349 g in 1 avoirdupois ounce (based on 16 oz/lb) and this ring contains 8.44 g of gold. The gold in the ring weighs 0.27 troy ounce or 0.30 avoirdupois oz. At $100 for the ring, that makes the price of the gold in the ring about $370 per troy ounce or $333 per avoirdupois ounce.

For Further Reading, Research, or Study

"Power Science—Will it Float?" *Science World,* vol. 49, no. 3 (Oct. 9, 1992), pp. 6–8.

This article contains a student experiment that gives one an excellent understanding of the concepts associated with items in this chapter.

Mebane, R., and Rybolt, T. *Adventures with Atoms and Molecules, Book II* (Hillside, N.J.: Enslow Publishers, 1985).

This book contains simple experiments concerning basic principles of chemistry, especially as they relate to atoms and molecules.

CHAPTER 8

THE WAVES OF NATURE

WHAT DO mosquitoes, bats, vision, and earthquakes have in common? This commonality may be important to you in solving the next few problems. Sound, light, and earthquakes can be described by waves that behave in the same fashion. There is an idea you may want to consider as you work toward solution of these items. How would you create a mosquito trap?

8.1 Ouch! Was That a Male or Female?

Explain how you would design experiments to answer the following questions: How can we determine what sound, if any, is emitted by mosquitoes?

How can we distinguish between male and female mosquitoes (Figure 8-1)? How can we demonstrate that sound is emitted by the female mosquito and that this sound is detected only by the male?

How can we determine which structure on the male mosquito detects sounds emitted by the female?

8.2 Here's One Way to Get Rid of Mosquitoes.

Design an experiment by which you could estimate the shortest wavelength of sound emitted by a bat (Figure 8-2). You might begin with the fact that when a 3.5 gram (g) bat was actually placed in a room containing mosquitoes, the

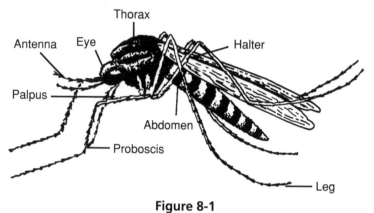

Figure 8-1

bat gained 0.4 g mass in 15 minutes by eating mosquitoes.

Assume that each mosquito is a small cubical solid, with a mass of 0.003 g, and an average density roughly one-fifth that of water.

Estimate the linear dimensions of the mosquito, and from that the lowest frequency of sound the bat must hear to detect the presence of the mosquito.

Figure 8-2

■Q 8.3 Waves of Vision.

The pupil of your eye (Figure 8-3) has a normal diameter of about 4 millimeters (it may dilate to as much as 8 mm in total darkness).

Suppose that you are on an airline trip when the airplane goes into its holding pattern, flying at some fixed altitude. You look down and see lots of people lying down on a beach (Figure 8-4).

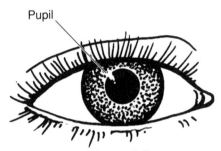

Pupil

Figure 8-3

Figure 8-4

If you can just distinguish two persons wearing bright red swimsuits lying next to each other, what is the maximum altitude of your airplane? If both of the two persons you can see lying next to each other are wearing bright blue swimsuits, what is the airplane's maximum altitude?

■Q 8.4 Watery Sight.

When you open your eyes underwater in a swimming pool, everything looks blurred, even when viewed by people with perfect vision. Yet when you put on a diving mask, everything is clear and distinct. How can this happen?

■Q 8.5 Shaky Waves.

Seismic waves produced by earthquakes or nuclear explosions on Earth do not follow straight-line paths as they move through the Earth. As shown in Figure 8-5, both the P (longitudinal) waves and the S (transverse) waves bend

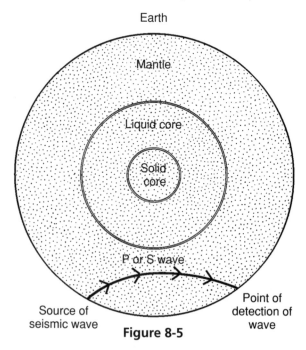

Figure 8-5

into semicircles as they pass into the Earth and back to some other point on the Earth.

How can you explain this phenomenon?

▌A 8.1 Ouch! Was That a Male or Female?

How can we distinguish male and female mosquitoes? We might first *define* a female mosquito as the one that produces eggs. Then we could isolate mosquitoes until we could observe the production of eggs. Once that had been done, then we would need to isolate some other mosquitoes, which produced no eggs.

Once we are confident about which is male and which is female, we could examine anatomical structures under a magnifying glass to see whether there were observable differences.

We would observe that in female mosquitoes, the antennae do not branch, and they look like sticks with a few small hairs (Figure 8-6).

To determine the sound emitted by female mosquitoes, we would need to record the female mosquito hum

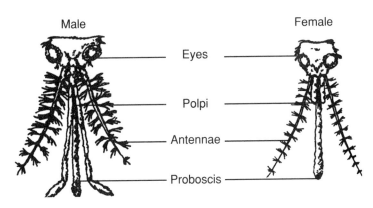

Male Female

Eyes

Polpi

Antennae

Proboscis

Figure 8-6

and try to isolate its cause and measure its frequency. The first person to do this was H. Maxim, the inventor of the machine gun. He had observed mosquitoes gathering around a humming transformer. They were all males. He then guessed (hypothesized) that they were being attracted by the hum, and that it must resemble the female's hum. By careful observation, it was seen that there was humming from a mosquito only when its wings were moving; thus a mosquito produces sound with its wings.

You should be able to set up experiments with tuning forks and mosquitoes to see what frequency is involved. You should be able to find ways to cover or hold fixed various parts of the mosquito, to find out which part must be detecting the humming sound. Through this process the antennae can be shown to be the detectors.

You should note the length of the small hairs on the antennae, since these detect the sounds. Those on the male are longer than those on the female. This means that the natural frequencies for the hairs on the male are lower than those for the female.

Observations and experiments then show that the male detects the sound produced by the female wings, which is between 500 and 550 hertz (Hz). The female's antennae hairs detect higher frequencies, more nearly 1,000 Hz, produced by wings of the male, and corresponding to a wavelength of about one-half that which the male detects. Notice that the hairs on the male antennae are about twice as long as those on the female.

■A 8.2 Here's One Way to Get Rid of Mosquitoes.

Humans can hear sounds with wavelengths from about 1 in to about 20 ft. If a bat is to "see" using sounds, then we know from diffraction of waves that the wavelength must be shorter than the objects (otherwise the sound wave bends around it, rather than forming a shadow, and giving a reflection) (Figure 8-7).

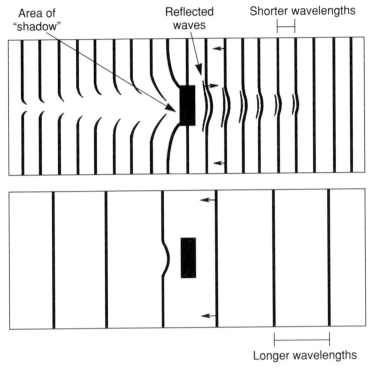

Area of "shadow"

Reflected waves

Shorter wavelengths

Longer wavelengths

Figure 8-7

A 1 in wavelength would mean that the bat could see very poorly. He or she would need a much shorter wavelength and, therefore, higher frequency.

If bats can eat enough mosquitoes in 15 min to increase their mass by 10%, they must see mosquitos awfully well. Thus the longest the wavelength could be is roughly the size of a mosquito. A 0.003 g mosquito having an average density of one-fifth that of water (0.2 g per cubic centimeter [g/cm³]) must occupy a volume of 0.015 cm³. If the mosquito is shaped like a small cube, its volume is W^3. Thus, 0.015 cm³ is the cube having the "size" or linear dimension "seen" by the bat. Taking the cube root of 0.015 cm³, we get about 2.5 mm, making the linear size of the mosquito about 2.5 mm.

Thus, if the bat is to see a mosquito, the wavelength of sound emitted must be less than 2.5 mm. Since frequency times wavelength equals wave speed, this would mean that the bat's sound frequency must be 330 meters/second (m/s) divided by 0.0025 m, the length of the mosquito in meters, or a minimum frequency of 130,000 Hz.

We might design an experiment by which successively smaller diameter wires are introduced into a bat cage. When the bat starts running into the wires, we know they are too small, and the diameter of the smallest wire they can "see" must be close to the shortest wavelength of sound emitted by the bat.

■A 8.3 Waves of Vision.

To solve this problem, you must understand the limits of resolution of light. When light travels from two points on some distant object and passes through an aperture of diameter D, light from each point diffracts, and together they produce an interference pattern. This pattern has a central maximum surrounded by minima on either side.

If the light from two points on some distant object produces interference patterns in such a way that the central maximum of the light from one point falls at the location of the first minimum of the pattern for the other point, the images produced will be merged in such a way that they cannot be distinguished from one another. The images of these two point sources cannot be resolved with light of that particular wavelength and an aperture of that size (Figure 8-8).

To determine an equation that fits the conditions just described, we might first start with each point source treated as if the light from each source travels in parallel rays to the aperture of diameter D. Then if the aperture is simplifed to be square, we can use the relationship for single slit diffraction, whose derivation is found in most elementary physics textbooks. By applying this relationship

90

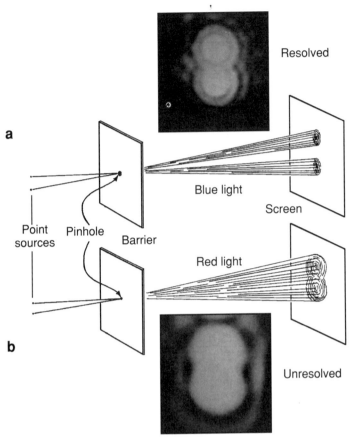

Figure 8-8

to both sources, looking at the first maximum of one source and the first minimum of the other source, you can derive a simple relationship given by $d=\lambda L/D$.

When the aperture is considered to be circular instead of rectangular, the result is only slightly different. Its derivation requires the use of more advanced mathematics. The minimum distance, d, between two point sources of light of wavelength, λ, that can be resolved from a distance L, with the light passing through an aperture of diameter D, is found to be $d=(1.22)\lambda L/D$.

In this problem, the light is red, which has a wavelength of about 700 nm. If we can see two persons lying next to each other, we must be able to resolve two red points separated by about 1 ft from the maximum altitude, L. Since the pupil of the eye has a diameter of about 4 mm, we can calculate that maximum altitude from which we could see these two persons in the red swimsuits.

We can use the equation $L=Dd/(1.22\lambda)$, or, in this case, $L=(1\ \text{ft})([4\ \text{mm}/(1.22 \times 0.0007\ \text{mm})]) = 4,700\ \text{ft}$.

If the people are wearing blue swimsuits, we can assume that the wavelength is about 400 nm. We need not use the equation. Since the distance, L, is inversely proportional to the wavelength, we can just multiply the result for red light by the quantity 7/4, giving an altitude of about 8,200 ft for blue swimsuits.

◼A 8.4 Watery Sight.

When you open your eyes underwater, the cornea of your eye is in contact with water. This means that the relative index of refraction of light passing directly from the water into your cornea and then into your eye lens has been made smaller. This would be the ratio of the index of refraction of the cornea and lens combination divided by the index of the water.

For air that ratio is the same as the index of refraction of your eye cornea and lens. But water has an index of refraction of 1.33, probably about the same as that of your eye cornea and lens. This has the effect of reducing or eliminating entirely the eye lens's ability to focus light.

When you put on a diving mask, the light passing through the transparent part of the mask is not bent. It is not a lens. Thus the light is not bent in passing through the mask. After that, the light is traveling in air—the air between your eye cornea and the mask. Thus the light can be bent by your eye lens in the same way as if you were in air instead of underwater.

■A 8.5 Shaky Waves.

As the depth below the surface of the Earth increases, so does the pressure. The density of solid material is largely unchanged even by large increases in pressure. But the rigidity or stiffness is changed. This rigidity increases with depth, and since the speed of the seismic waves increases with rigidity or stiffness, there is an increase in the velocity of the seismic waves with increasing depths into Earth.

The speed of P waves (longitudinal waves) increases from about 5 kilometers/second (km/s) near the Earth's surface to about 1,300 km/s at a depth of 2,400 km. The speed of S waves (transverse waves) increases from about 3 km/s near the Earth's surface to about 7 km/s at 2,400 km depth.

You will remember that when light enters a medium like glass, the light rays bend toward the normal because the light waves slow down. When the light leaves the glass and enters air again, the light rays bend away from the normal because they are traveling faster.

In the same way, when a seismic wave passes from a medium in which it travels at a certain speed to another medium in which the speed is greater, the wave direction bends away from the normal to that surface. In this case the medium, the Earth, is continuously changing in such a way that the seismic wave speed also changes continuously.

Instead of an abrupt bending away from the normal to the boundary between two places where the wave is observed, there is a steady bending away from that normal as the wave moves into the Earth, where its speed steadily increases with depth.

As the wave reaches its greatest depth and begins to move toward the surface again, its speed decreases as it decreases depth. Under these conditions, the wave direction tends to bend continuously toward the normal. This has the effect of continuing the curved path it had taken as it penetrated downward into the Earth.

For Further Reading, Research, or Study

Malin, D. "A Universe of Color," *Scientific American*, vol. 269, no. 2 (August 1993), pp. 72–77.

This article uses color photography as an astronomical tool. It shows that celestial objects have details not yet captured by modern electronics detectors. The article describes how certain wavelengths of color reveal aspects of the universe.

Parkfield Working Group "Parkfield: First Short-Term Earthquake Warning," *Earth in Space*, vol. 5, no. 8 (April 1993), pp. 5–7.

This article describes the development of the Parkfield Earthquake Prediction Experiment. The article offers interesting aspects of earthquake warning systems, and how the science of waves applies to such phenomena. Earthquake prediction appears to be advancing dramatically, and this article provides information on techniques used for such prediction.

Bolt, B. *Inside the Earth* (San Francisco: W. H. Freeman and Co., 1982), chap. 2.

This book, by Bruce Bolt, is the best general reference concerning the physical properties of the material inside our Earth. It provides a detailed examination of the various kinds of earthquake waves, seismology, and the most current view of the Earth's interior. Mathematics is kept relatively simple, mainly through the use of algebra.

CHAPTER 9

BOBBING IN AIR

JUST LIKE WATER, the air can buoy objects, and, depending on certain characteristics of the objects, some may sink or float in air. In the next set of items, air is the fluid. One interesting historical item you may want to investigate after you have solved these problems is the *Hindenburg*, how it was buoyed, and why it burned and crashed in Lakehurst, New Jersey.

■Q 9.1 Balloon Science.

A helium-filled balloon, which does not contain so much helium that it stretches the balloon, is just barely able to lift an 80 kilogram (kg) girl off the ground. The empty balloon has a mass of 5 kg (Figure 9-1).

Suppose that the helium in the balloon is replaced by hydrogen gas occupying exactly the same volume. How much more or less can be lifted when it contains the hydrogen gas? Explain your reasoning.

■Q 9.2 Massy Air.

A block of balsa wood and a block of lead are taken aboard a spacecraft to Earth's moon. An astronaut uses a very accurate and precise balance to measure the mass of each of these blocks on the surface of the moon. The block of balsa wood is found to have a mass of exactly 500.00 grams (g). From its dimensions, the astronaut determines

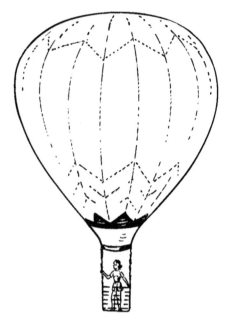

Figure 9-1

the volume of the block and, knowing its mass, calculates its density, 0.125 grams/cubic centimeter (g/cm³). In the same way, the lead block is found also to have a mass of exactly 500.00 g and a density of 11.4 g/cm³. These two blocks are then taken back to Earth, and the balsa wood block is placed on one pan of a very precise and accurate equal arm balance. The lead block is placed on the other pan (Figure 9-2).

Before adding the blocks, the balance is carefully set level and is located at a place on Earth where the density of air is 1.30 g/1000 cm³. It is observed that in spite of the fact that these two masses are identical and the balance is precise and accurate, one of these two blocks will not balance the other block unless additional mass is added to one side of the balance.

Explain carefully why this is true; then calculate how

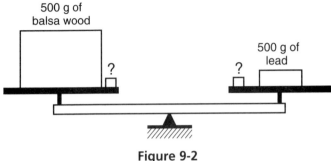

Figure 9-2

much mass must be added to produce an observable "balance," stating on which side it must be added, and why.

What does this result tell you about errors associated with precise measurements of chemicals with a microbalance on Earth?

■◗ 9.3 Air Holding Up Air?

A student wanted to determine the density of air. He carefully prepared a balance consisting of a meter stick, with the fulcrum at the 50 centimeter (cm) mark. Then at the 10 cm mark and the 90 cm mark he placed holders for his balance. In this way they were equally spaced from the fulcrum, and any mass on the unknown side could be found just by balancing it with known standard masses on the other side. An empty balloon was placed on one side and masses on the other side to achieve a balance. Then the balloon was inflated with air (Figure 9-3).

He reasoned that a balloon that is inflated will weigh less than the same balloon not inflated because the inflated balloon displaces air, thus producing a buoyancy force upward, whereas the balloon that is not inflated does not do so. The difference in these two mass measurements would be the mass of the displaced air.

Finding the volume of the balloon would allow the volume of the displaced air to be known. Then the den-

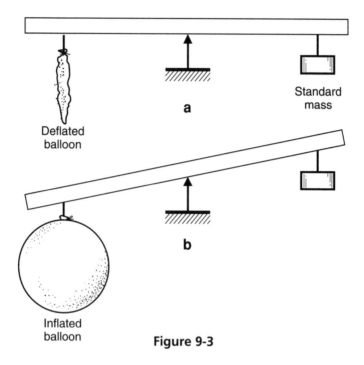

Figure 9-3

sity of air could be calculated. He carried out the measurements, but the results were opposite to what he expected. The balloon of mass 2.325 g without air in it had a mass of 2.400 g when it was inflated. How do you account for this discrepancy?

▰A 9.1 Balloon Science.

Helium gas, which is monatomic, has an atomic mass of 4 g/mole, and hydrogen gas, which is diatomic, has a molecular mass of 2 g/mole. The total mass of helium gas in the balloon is therefore twice that of the hydrogen gas when the balloon is filled to the same volume.

There is a temptation to jump quickly to the conclusion that the lift will be twice as great with hydrogen as with helium. But is this correct? Archimedes' principle states that the buoyancy force on some object immersed in a fluid is equal to the weight of the fluid displaced.

In this case the fluid displaced is air, and the volume of air displaced is the same in both cases. Thus the buoyancy force is exactly the same for both hydrogen and helium gases. But we know that hydrogen has greater lift than helium. So why is this, and how much more can be lifted by hydrogen gas? The buoyancy force is the same, but what the balloon must lift is different.

In the case of the helium-filled balloon, it must lift the balloon (5 kg mass), the girl (80 kg), and the helium itself. The hydrogen-filled balloon must lift some mass M (which we believe is greater than 80 kg), the mass of the balloon itself, and the hydrogen gas.

The question is reduced to finding how the weight ratio of helium to hydrogen compares with the weight of an equal volume of air. We know that air is composed of some 21% oxygen, 78% nitrogen, and about 1% other gases, with argon dominant at about 0.9%. Since oxygen has a molecular mass of 32 g/mole, nitrogen 28 g/mole, and argon 40 g/mole, we can use the percentage compositions to find the weighted average molecular mass for air (0.78 x 28 + 0.21 x 32 + 0.01 x 40). This gives a result of about 29 g/mole.

Since for equal volumes the molecular masses of the gases give direct measures of their densities and weights, we can just look at these differences. For a helium-filled balloon, we would have 29 g/mole minus 4 g/mole, or a "lift" of 25 g/mole. In the case of hydrogen, the "lift" is 29 g/mole minus 2 g/mole, or a "lift" of 27 g/mole. Thus the hydrogen gas will lift only 27/25 =1.08 times more than a helium-filled balloon of equal volume.

We would expect an 8% increase in total lift for the balloon. Since the helium-filled balloon lifted 80 kg (girl) plus 5 kg (empty balloon), the hydrogen-filled balloon will lift 8% more, or a total of 91.8 kg. Since the balloon accounts for 5 kg of this mass, the actual load that can be lifted is 86.8 kg, or 6.8 kg more than the helium-filled balloon would lift. The reasoning used in this answer eliminated the need to solve equations. However, the same problem can be solved by a straightforward use of equations involving densities, volumes, molecular masses, and numbers of moles of the gases. But the latter solution is far more complicated in its appearance.

This is a good example of where careful reasoning can produce easier solutions.

■A 9.2 Massy Air.

This is another problem requiring an understanding of Archimedes' principle. But this problem has very important implications for chemists, who want to obtain very precise mass measurements of low-density materials with precision balances.

When we weigh something, usually a solid, on a balance, we ignore the fact that the solid is immersed in an ocean of air. That air provides a buoyancy force upward, which makes the mass reading on a balance lower than it should be.

A 500 g block of balsa wood of density 0.125 g/cm^3 has a volume (using density D=M/V in the form V=M/D), V, of 4,000 cm^3. The lead weight used to balance the balsa wood has a density of 11.4 g/cm^3. Its volume must be just 43.9 cm^3. The 500 g balsa wood block must displace 4,000/43.9, or 91.1 times more air than the lead weight. The buoyancy force on the balsa block must therefore be 91.1 times greater than the buoyancy force acting on the lead weight.

Since the air has a density of 0.00130 g/cm^3, in the case of balsa, there must be 4,000 x 0.00130, or 5.20 g, of air displaced. For the lead weight, there would be only

43.9 x 0.00130, or 0.06 g, of air displaced. For the effects of buoyancy to be corrected, we must place an additional 5.14 g (the buoyancy force on this small piece of lead is quite negligible compared with the other values, so it may be ignored) of lead on the side of the balance with the block of balsa wood. This will allow the system to be in balance.

You can see that when you are making precise mass measurements, you do need to take buoyancy into account. This could be done most easily by using a known mass of the same substance on one side of the balance as is used as the unknown mass on the other side. Electronic and single pan balances rely on standard masses for calibration. Those standard masses are usually heavy metal; thus you still need to adjust for buoyancy when you want precise mass measurements.

◼A 9.3 Air Holding up Air?

The standard masses for this balance are not balancing just the mass of the balloon minus the buoyant force of the air displaced. The balloon has air in it. If there is no stretch of the balloon, the air in the balloon, by virtue of its weight, exerts a force downward exactly equal to the buoyant force of the air displaced.

When the balloon is stretched, the air inside must be compressed, making it heavier than the air that is displaced. Thus when the balloon is inflated, it will weigh slightly more than an empty balloon. This, of course, is what was observed.

This attempt to weigh the balloon and find by this method the density or weight of air is defective. This procedure, although frequently used by teachers to demonstrate that air has weight, does not illustrate that point at all. It merely shows that compressed air weighs more than air that is not compressed. The demonstration certainly does not show buoyancy effects, since they are completely eliminated by the fact that the balloon material occupies almost no volume by which it can displace air, and it is only the air inside displacing air outside which eliminates buoyancy as a factor.

For Further Reading, Research, or Study

Zubrowski, B. *Messing Around with Baking Chemistry: A Children's Museum Activity Book* (Boston: Little Brown and Co., 1981).

This book presents experiments and projects that explore what happens when batter and dough turn into cake and bread. The book emphasizes the physical and biochemical properties of baking powder, baking soda, and yeast. The experiments use simple items from the home kitchen.

Kaner, E., with illustrations by Phillips, L. *Balloon Science* (Reading, Mass.: Addison-Wesley Publishing Co., 1989).

This book provides a collection of well-illustrated balloon experiments, activities, games, riddles, and interesting and surprising facts about balloons. In the process, the properties of air are looked at in a variety of situations.

Aldridge, B., Waldman, G., and Arons, A. *Analytical Balance: A Module on Measurement, Errors, and Mechanical Equilibrium* (New York: McGraw-Hill, 1975. Available from the American Association of Physics Teachers, College Park, Md.), Section C.

This module has an excellent treatment of the buoyancy correction for balances. It also provides one of the best discussions of Archimedes' principle that can be found. It offers a number of interesting experiments that can lead to research projects.

Gardner, R. *Ideas for Science Projects* (New York: Franklin Watts, 1986), pp. 59–60, "Weighing Gases."

This book offers many good ideas for projects, and this article describes in detail how to weigh gases, including weighing the air.

CHAPTER 10

DRUNK MOLECULES?

SOLIDS, LIQUIDS, AND GASES move in interesting ways. The obvious, familiar ways involve huge numbers of molecules flowing or moving together. But what about the submicroscopic motion? Here, the motion is completely random, like that of a "drunk molecule." How do those random motions connect to what we can observe and measure? The next few items will explore such questions.

■Q 10.1 Hard Eggs Without Cooking.

Many food stores sell pickled eggs. These eggs appear to be hard-boiled. Somehow, the liquid interiors have been changed to become solid. To make pickled eggs, unopened raw eggs are placed in a salty solution, and over a short period of time they turn into hard-boiled pickled eggs.

How can this transformation occur?

■Q 10.2 Give Me My Space.

Air has a density of 1.29 grams/liter (g/l) at 0°C and one atmosphere of pressure. Air consists of about 21% oxygen (32 g/mole), 78% nitrogen (28 g/mole), and 0.9% argon (40 g/mole). The other 0.1% is made up of other inert gases and carbon dioxide. The average mass of a mole of air, which is calculated from a weighted average of the masses of a mole of each of these gases, is 28.95 g.

Now consider the liquid, water. Water has a molecular

mass of 18 g/mole and a density of 1.00 grams/cubic centimeter (g/cm^3). We know that a mole contains Avogadro's number, N_o, of molecules, where $N_o = 6.025 \times 10^{23}$.

How much volume is occupied by a water molecule? What is the average distance separating water molecules? How much volume is occupied by the average "air" molecule? What is the average distance between "air" molecules? How many times greater is this separation than that for water molecules?

■Q 10.3 Don't Block My Way!

The *vapor pressure* of water is the pressure associated with the evaporation of water from its surface. Water will evaporate until the vapor pressure of the water remaining is equal to the vapor pressure of water in the air above the liquid water. Then the number of water molecules leaving the surface per unit of time is equal to the number of water molecules entering the surface. This is an equilibrium condition.

While the water is evaporating with a net loss of liquid water, the effect is to lower the temperature of the liquid water that remains. When this effect is observed for a solution of sugar water in which there is 1 sugar molecule for every 10 water molecules, and this result is compared with that of a solution of salt water having 1 sodium chloride molecule for every 10 water molcules, it is found that both solutions evaporate more slowly than regular water. The reduction in evaporation rate for salt water is observed to be twice what it is for sugar water.

Why is the evaporation rate lower for these solutions, and how can you explain this difference in evaporation rates between the salt solution and the sugar solution?

■Q 10.4 Make Room for One More?

What is wrong with the following explanation? When you have air over water, the amount of water vapor in the air increases with the temperature. As air is heated, it expands. When air expands, the molecules are farther apart on the average than at lower temperatures.

Since the molecules are farther apart, there is more room for additional water molecules, and the air can therefore hold more water.

Analyze this explanation in terms of the kinetic-molecular theory of gases.

■Q 10.5 What Holds It Up?

Suppose that on a day when the temperature is 25°C and the atmospheric pressure is 760 millimeters of mercury (mm Hg), a graduated cylinder is filled almost completely with water and carefully placed into a large beaker of water as shown in Figure 10-1a.

This is done without allowing additional air into the cylinder as it is being inverted and placed onto spacers on the bottom of the beaker. (This allows water to enter or leave the cylinder from the beaker.) Next a pump is used to take water out of the beaker. Water is taken out of the beaker until it appears as shown in Figure 10-1b.

If we had filled the graduated cylinder with water, with no air spaces, and if we were able to place it into the beaker without any air getting inside the cylinder, what would have been the level of water in the cylinder before water was pumped out of the beaker?

How do you explain this answer?

We actually did allow some air into the graduated cylinder before placing it into the beaker. Under those conditions the water level in the graduated cylinder was 5 centimeters (cm) above the beaker water surface before pumping and 15 cm above that surface after pumping. The air space in the graduated cylinder was initially 10 cm. Then when the water was pumped out of the beaker, the water level in the graduated cylinder dropped, but only by some small amount Δh.

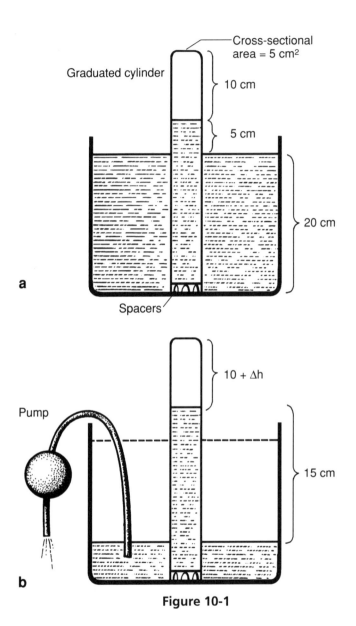

Figure 10-1

How can you explain why the water level falls such a small amount? And what is the approximate value of Δh?

■A 10.1 Hard Eggs Without Cooking.

Eggs are very porous. They need to be porous to allow oxygen to move in and carbon dioxide to move out of the hard outer shell. Not only can gases move in and out, but so can some liquids.

If you examine with a magnifying glass the shell of an egg, you will see that it has many tiny openings or pores. In the question, these openings allowed the briny solution to enter the egg and turn the raw egg into a hard egg. But the more viscous, gelatinous substance of the egg white cannot pass through the pores. Molecules easily move back and forth, so that a fertilized egg can exchange gases with the air, as the embryonic chick develops.

■A 10.2 Give Me My Space.

A mole of water molecules must occupy a volume of $V=M/\rho$, where M is the molecular mass in grams/mole (g/mole) and ρ is the density in grams/cubic centimeter (g/cm³). In this case we have (18 g/mole)/(1.00 g/cm³), or 18 cm³/mole.

Now that we know how much volume is occupied by a mole of water molecules, we can divide by Avogadro's number to find the volume of a single molecule. Thus, we have that volume as (18 cm³/mole)/(6.025 x 10²³ molecules/mole), which gives a result of 2.99 x 10⁻²³cm³/molecule, which can be written 29.9 x 10⁻²⁴ cm³/molecule. Let us assume that this volume is a cube of side length L. Then we can find L by taking the cube root of this volume.

This can most easily be done by finding the logarithm of the number 29.9, dividing by 3, then find the antilog. This gives us 3.10 for that part of the cube root. The cube root of the exponential is easy. We just divide the exponent by 3. Thus we get, 3.10×10^{-8} cm = L. This is the average separation of molecules of water.

Now what about air molecules? A mole of air at standard temperature and pressure (STP) would occupy 22.4 l, a fact we know from chemistry. But let's see whether that is true from our given information. We find (28.95 g/mole)/(1.29×10^{-3} g/cm³), which gives the result 22,400 cm³/mole.

Now we can find the volume of one molecule by dividing by how many molecules are in this volume, Avogadro's number.

Thus we have (22,400 cm³/mole)/(6.025×10^{23} molecules/mole), which gives a result of 37.2×10^{-21} cm³/molecule, as the volume occupied by the average air molecule.

Now all we need to do is take the cube root of this volume to find the side length L of the cube in which the average air molecule can be found. Taking that cube root, we have L = 3.34×10^{-7} cm. Now, how much farther apart are air molecules than water molecules? We need only divide the distance (3.34×10^{-7} cm) by (3.10×10^{-8} cm),

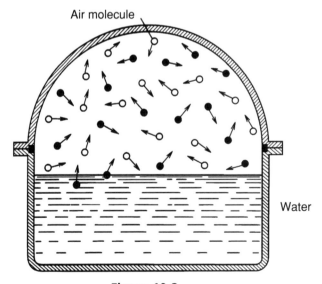

Air molecule

Water

Figure 10-2

which gives the factor 11. Thus air molecules are 11 times farther apart than water molecules (Figure 10-2).

▪A 10.3 Don't Block My Way!

First let's consider the fact that the evaporation rate is decreased when sugar or salt is added to water. Why does this happen? When you have a solution of sugar water, there are sugar molecules mixed in among the water molecules. The surface of the water therefore has fewer water molecules than before, since some of the surface consists of sugar molecules.

This means fewer water molecules are available to leave the surface, and the rate of evaporation will decrease. Similarly, the temperature of the water is not lowered so much, since fewer molecules are carrying energy away from the water.

But why would an equal concentration of salt water reduce the amount of evaporation twice as much as for sugar water? Sugar water has single sugar molecules, but salt does not enter water as molecules. Salt dissociates into sodium ions and chloride ions. These ions take up space just as molecules do. Therefore, the 10% salt solution is the equivalent of a 20% sugar solution in terms of numbers of particles that can occupy spaces otherwise occupied by water molecules (Figure 10-3).

Thus the rate of evaporation is reduced twice as much for this salt solution as for the sugar solution.

▪A 10.4 Make Room for One More?

The problem with this explanation is that it does not correctly explain how water molecules enter air. Even though molecules of air are farther apart at higher temperatures, this has nothing to do with the amount of water the air can hold.

You know this from your own experience. If you are in a bathroom with a shower that has been turned on with

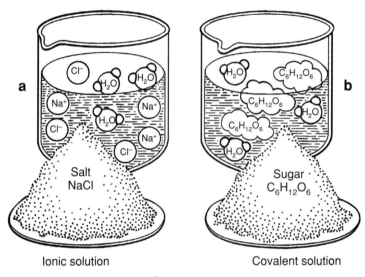

a   b

Ionic solution   Covalent solution

Figure 10-3

very hot water, the room can be quite saturated with water vapor. Water will not evaporate from your body very quickly, even though the room temperature is quite high and, therefore, the air molecules must be very far apart. On the other hand, if you walk into a bedroom that is very cold, but in which there is very little water vapor, your body will dry very quickly. Yet in this cold room, the air molecules are closer together than in the hot bathroom. It is not the spacing of the air molecules that determines how much water can be added to the air: It is entirely the temperature of the water and whether that liquid water is in equilibrium with water vapor in the air.

    At normal temperatures and pressures, the interaction of air molecules with each other is irrelevant to the pressure the air exerts. Also, water molecules added to air produce a pressure quite independent of the pressure from the air molecules. The sum of these pressures is the total pressure. It is the interaction of the molecules of air and water with the surfaces of their container or the surface of water inside the container that produces pressure.

When water evaporates, molecules leave the surface and enter the air above it. This process is determined by the vapor pressure of the water, which depends upon the temperature of the water. As the number of molecules leaving the water increases, more and more are contained within the air above. Many of these return to the water. When the rate at which molecules of water evaporate is equal to the rate at which they return to the water, we say that the air is *saturated* for that temperature and pressure.

If you increase the air pressure on water, the number of water molecules leaving the surface actually increases, rather than decreasing as you would expect if it were the spacing of air molecules that made it possible to add more water to air.

■A 10.5 What Holds It Up?

If the cylinder had been completely filled with water, with no air present, then the only pressure exerted inside the cylinder would have been the column of water in the cylinder measured above the level of the water in the beaker. But the pressure pushing back on this column of water is due to the weight of the earth's atmosphere.

We know that on this particular day the atmosphere will balance a column of mercury 760 mm high. Since mercury is 13.6 times more dense than water, the atmosphere should balance a column of water that is 13.6 times 760 mm, or about 10,300 mm H_2O. However, water evaporates off the surface of water in the cylinder and exerts a pressure. This vapor pressure for water is about 23.7 mm Hg at 25°C. (This 23.7 mm Hg would just balance 23.7 x 13.6 mm of water; thus 23.7 mm Hg is equivalent to 322 mm H_2O.) In contrast, the vapor pressure of mercury at this temperature is only about 0.002 mm Hg, a negligible amount compared with that of water. Thus, the vapor pressure of the water adds to the water column a pressure equivalent to about 300 mm, thus requiring a column of water of only about 10,000 mm to balance the atmosphere.

This is 1,000 cm, 394 in, or about 33 ft of water. Thus, before you could fill a graduated cylinder with water, invert it, and expect to see any empty space at the top without water in it, the column would have to be more than 33 ft high.

This fact was well known to the ancients, who saw that you could not pump water out of deep wells or mines except by doing so in stages, where the pumps would pump considerably less than 33 ft at a time.

The situation where we allowed some air above the water column in the cylinder relates directly to the way that inverted bottle feeders are used to provide water to poultry or to provide sugar water to hummingbirds (Figure 10-4). In

Figure 10-4

this case, there was an initial column 10 cm high, and the cylinder had an inside cross-sectional area of 5 cm². Thus the initial volume of the air was 10 cm x 5 cm² = 50 cm³.

The initial pressure acting on this volume was the atmospheric pressure, which will balance 1,000 cm of water minus the 5 cm of water in the cylinder, but above the level of the beaker water. Thus the initial pressure was equivalent to a column of 995 cm of water.

When we pumped out the water, the pressure acting on the air pocket inside the cylinder had been reduced by a column of an additional 10 cm of water. Thus the pressure on the gas pocket was such that it would balance a column of 985 cm of water. You know the initial volume and pressure and the final pressure.

From Boyle's law, $P_1V_1 = P_2V_2$, you can calculate the final volume. In this case it must be found from 995 cm x 50 cm³ = 985 cm x [(10 cm + Δh) x 5 cm²]. Solving for Δh, we have Δh = 0.1 cm, or 1 mm.

For Further Reading, Research, or Study

Mebane, R., and Rybolt, T., *Adventures with Atoms and Molecules* (Hillside, N.J.: Enslow Publishers, 1985).

This book contains numerous simple experiments relating to atoms and molecules. Many are experiments that can be done at home. It is a rich source of chemical research and application ideas.

De Vito, A. *Teaching with Eggs* (West Lafayette, Ind.: Creative Ventures, 1982).

This nice little book contains a series of experiments and stories using chicken eggs. Eggs are great devices for study of physical and biological principles, and the book offers a number of interesting uses in the study of science.

Bohren, C. *Clouds in a Glass of Beer: Simple Experiments in Atmospheric Physics* (New York: John Wiley & Sons, 1987), chap. 6.

This is an excellent book for the student who wants to clear up misconceptions or better understand the science associated with atmospheric physics. The book is filled with ideas that could lead to interesting science projects or research.

CHAPTER 11

HEATING UP THE SITUATION

HEAT is one of those very peculiar concepts. People often confuse it with temperature. Heat isn't an object; you cannot see it. Can you feel it? Or is it something else you feel? Would a house with walls filled with water be better insulated than a brick house? The following items explore some of these questions.

■Q 11.1 Water for Insulation?

The *thermal conductivity* of a substance is a measure of its ability to conduct heat. In engineering units, the constant associated with thermal conductivities is expressed in units of British thermal unit-inches/square foot-hours-degrees Fahrenheit (Btu–in/ft²–hr–°F). The thermal conductivities of several common substances are as follows: rock wool 0.28, corkboard 0.27, cinder blocks 2.5, glass 5.0, copper 236, and water 0.35.

The larger the number associated with one of these substances, the more that heat is conducted through that material in a given time with a given area, thickness, and temperature difference. Since water has such a low value of thermal conductivity, why couldn't we use water as an insulator, placing it in spaces between the walls of a house, rather than using much more expensive materials?

Why is it that in a "weightless" environment water would be a good heat insulator?

■Q 11.2 Energetic Air?

According to the kinetic-molecular theory of ideal gases, a gas containing diatomic molecules will have a molar specific heat (at constant volume) of 20.79 joules/mole-Kelvin (J/mole-K). Thus when the temperature of 1 mole of a typical diatomic gas drops 1° Celsius (also 1 K), 20.79 joules of energy is released.

Oxygen and nitrogen are both diatomic molecules in air, and the combination of nitrogen and oxygen accounts for about 99% of air molecules.

An inventor claims that he has devised a machine that takes in air at room temperature (27° C, and 300 K) at the rate of 1,000 moles per second, extracts energy from the air, and returns it to the surroundings when the air is at a temperature of 200 K (−73° C). This means that the invention somehow extracts 2,079,000 joules of energy per second from the air. This is 2,079 kilowatts (kW) of power (Figure 11-1).

Is this invention consistent with the law of conservation of energy? Is it possible for such a machine actually to work as described? If not, explain carefully why such an invention cannot work.

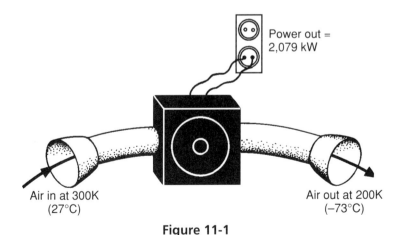

Power out = 2,079 kW

Air in at 300K (27°C)

Air out at 200K (−73°C)

Figure 11-1

Figure 11-2

■Q **11.3 Monetary Aeronautics.**

Hold the edge of one end of a dollar bill against your lower lip. Then very gently blow puffs of air downward along the top outward surface of the dollar bill (Figure 11-2).

What do you observe? Explain this observation in terms of the kinetic-molecular theory of gases.

■Q **11.4 Two Gases and a Spark.**

Six milliliters (ml) of hydrogen gas having a mass of 0.535 mg is mixed with 6 ml of oxygen having a mass of 8.56 mg. The two gases, both at standard temperature and pressure, are contained in a sealed chamber in which an electric spark can be produced.

When the mixture is ignited, there is a small explosion in the chamber and drops of water are observed to result from the reaction. How many milliliters of hydrogen react? How many milliliters of oxygen? How many milligrams of hydrogen react? How many milligrams of oxygen? How many milligrams of water are produced?

What empirical laws of chemistry are exemplified by this reaction? Describe how you arrive at your results in terms of the atomic and molecular theories of matter.

◼Q 11.5 Sunshine Heat?

There is a common belief that sunlight heats the air around us. But direct sunlight does not account for the warm air during the day or the cool air at night. How is the air heated and cooled if not directly by sunlight? And what is the evidence that the sunlight does not directly heat the air?

◼A 11.1 Water for Insulation?

It may be a great surprise to you to learn that water conducts heat so poorly. In fact, water is almost as good an insulator (at .35) as corkboard (.27) or rockwool (.28).

Water is a much better insulator than glass (at 5.0) or cinderblock (at 2.5). Now why can't we use water as an insulator? The answer is simple. Water is a liquid, and its molecules can move past each other with great ease, while all of these other substances are solids, in which the molecules do not move around.

When water is heated, it expands. This occurs because the molecules vibrate at greater rates at higher temperatures. This makes the average distance between molecules greater, which means that the density of the water decreases when it is hotter. Low-density water rises, while high-density water sinks. This is called *convection*. As a result of convection, water can carry heat from one surface to another.

Thus, even though water is a very poor conductor of heat, it will transfer heat by convection quite readily. This is the reason water cannot be used as a heat insulator. In a weightless environment, however, convection cannot occur. Therefore, water would make an excellent insulator of heat in a weightless environment. One might argue that since water has such a high specific heat (it holds more heat than most substances), it would absorb much heat and therefore would not make such a good insulator. While it is true that water would absorb much heat initially, that heat would also be given up quite slowly. In this sense, the water serves as a buffer, slowing the rate at which the interior temperature can change. This is why climates are more moderate around large bodies of water.

■A 11.2 Energetic Air?

This is a typical example of a perpetual motion machine of the second kind. Perpetual motion machines of the first kind are those for which claims are made that you can get more energy out of some device than can be put into it. This violates the law of conservation of energy.

But perpetual motion machines of the second kind do not violate the law of conservation of energy. Indeed, they look quite plausible. In this case, for example, 1,000 moles of air at room temperature certainly does contain energy. And if the temperature of this air is lowered by 100 K degrees, there will be 2,079,000 joules of energy released.

But such a device is impossible for another reason. It violates the second law of thermodynamics. For a machine to function as described, heat would need to flow from cold to hot, but heat only flows from a hotter body to a colder body.

In reality, the maximum efficiency of any heat engine is determined entirely by the temperature difference between the engine's working substance and the reservoir with which it is coupled.

■A 11.3 Monetary Aeronautics.

You are blowing gentle puffs of air past one side of the dollar bill. Air on the other side is still. The dollar bill moves

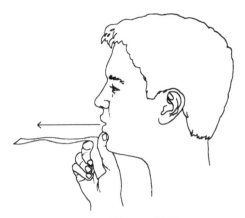

Figure 11-3

outward. This can only happen if the air pressure on the underside of the dollar bill is higher than the air pressure on the side along which you are blowing (Figure 11-3).

Normally, about a third (since there are three directions possible) of the molecules in a sample of air would be hitting the dollar bill over some short interval of time. This should happen equally on both sides of the dollar bill. Now why is the air pressure less on one side than on the other side?

Let us apply what we know of the kinetic-molecular theory of gases. By blowing along one side, large numbers of the air molecules on that side are given velocities that are directed mainly parallel to the surface of the dollar bill. This means that fewer than one-third of the molecules on that side are impinging perpendicularly upon the dollar bill's surface over a given short time interval.

On the other side of the dollar bill, where the air is still, one-third of the molecules in the same size sample of air continue to strike the other surface. Thus, there is a net excess force or pressure on that side of the bill, and it moves outward.

▰A 11.4 Two Gases and a Spark.

This item requires an understanding of chemical reactions. Students often memorize chemical formulas and are required to show how much mass or volume is needed in such reactions. Seldom must they consider a problem in which there is an excess of one substance over another.

In this case there is an excess of oxygen gas. From the atomic theory of Dalton, and the empirical laws of definite proportions and combining volumes, we know that 2 volumes of hydrogen gas combine chemically with 1 volume of oxygen gas. Since there is 6 ml of hydrogen gas, the reaction will need at most 3 ml of oxygen gas, leaving 3 ml of oxygen unused. Hydrogen reacts with oxygen in a mass ratio of 1 to 8.

This was observed empirically before theory would have predicted it from the relative atomic masses of these elements. According to theory, 2 atoms of oxygen have a molecular mass of 32 and 2 atoms of hydrogen have a molecular mass of 2. But there are 2 volumes of hydrogen for each volume of oxygen in the reaction, thus we need 4 mass units of hydrogen for each 32 mass units of oxygen, giving a ratio of 1 to 8. Since all of the hydrogen will be consumed in the reaction, 0.535 mg of hydrogen will burn. Since only half of the oxygen is consumed, the reaction requires only 4.28 mg of oxygen (a ratio of 1 to 8 by mass).

From this reaction about 4.82 mg of water will be produced. This item tests for *understanding* of very basic chemistry. If you answer this item incorrectly but can write the chemical equation for the reaction, you do not really understand the underlying principles or concepts which are being summarized by the more abstract expression of an equation.

▰A 11.5 Sunshine Heat.

Suppose that sunlight were the main way in which air is heated during the day and cooled at night. Then we would expect the temperature of the air to increase with altitude during the day and decrease with altitude during nighttime when the air is cooling. But that is the reverse of what actually happens.

During the daytime, the temperature of the air decreases with altitude, and at night the temperature of the air cools off first near the ground. This can only be because the sunlight is absorbed mainly by the Earth's surface and reradiated as heat, warming the air during the daytime. At night, as the Earth cools off, it cools the air closest to the ground first. And this is what we observe.

For Further Reading, Research, or Study

Falk, D. "A Good Brain Is Hard to Cool," *Natural History,* vol. 102, no. 8 (August 1993), p. 65.

This is a very interesting article on how the human skull serves as a radiator for the brain. It connects physics and physiology in important ways. The article offers several interesting areas for possible student research. This issue of *Natural History* is entirely devoted to heat, so it offers a wealth of additional ideas.

Stinchecum, A. "Cool Illusions in the Land of the Rising Sun,"*Natural History,* vol. 102, no. 8 (August 1993), p. 60.

This article explains how appearances affect our sensation of heat. The article looks carefully at heat and how different materials can best be used to assist the body in temperature regulation. It does so in unusual and interesting ways.

CHAPTER 12

FORCEFUL PROBLEMS

CAN REAL LIFE DECISIONS depend upon physics? You bet they can. Some of these items are examples. Who do I want to tackle me in football? How can I do less work than someone else? Can I really move thousands of pounds? See how you do in answering some of these questions.

■Q 12.1 Log Lifting Contest.

Three people are going to lift and carry horizontally a uniformly thick 10 ft log weighing 300 lb. One person lifts an end of the log, and the other two persons lift at the same place, one across the log from the other, at some distance from the other end of the log (Figure 12-1).

Where must these two persons lift the log if each of them is to lift 120 lb, and the person at the end of the log is to lift 60 lb?

■Q 12.2 Science Tips for Boaters.

A boater brings his 2 ton boat near the shore, the bow forward, the starboard side of the boat close to a dock of a small uninhabited island (Berkeley Island on the Piankatank River) just off the Chesapeake Bay. He stays overnight, expecting to depart the following morning in time to get back to his marina, drive home, and make an afternoon flight on a business trip.

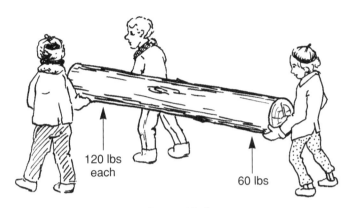

120 lbs
each

60 lbs

Figure 12-1

The next morning he discovers that the tide is out, his boat is now grounded, and he may have to wait 3 or 4 hours and miss his flight. As he ponders his quandary, he remembers something he learned in physics class years before. He then ties a line (a rope to those who are not sailors) from the bow of the boat to a piling located at the end of the pier just beyond the stern on the starboard side of the boat (Figure 12-2).

He is then able to move the boat until it is finally free, and he is on his way, without further difficulty. What did he do? And what physics principle did he take advantage of

Figure 12-2

that made it possible to exert such a huge force that he could slide a 4,000 lb boat off the sand and into the deeper water?

■Q 12.3 To Brake or Not to Brake.

You are riding in a car with the gear shift in neutral. The car is coasting from 60 mph to a stop at the top of a hill. The hill is inclined 30° with the horizontal. The car slows down until it finally stops, the speedometer showing exactly 0 mph (Figure 12-3).

Just as the speedometer reads zero, you put your foot on the brake. At that instant, how much gravitational force (g) along the incline will you be experiencing?

Suppose instead that the car were slowly coasting to a stop when it was moving along a perfectly level, horizontal road (Figure 12-4).

How many g's of force along the horizontal do you experience at the instant when the car's speedometer reads 0 mph and you have just put your foot on the brake?

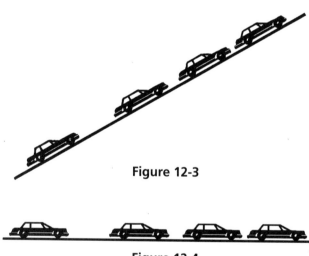

Figure 12-3

Figure 12-4

■Q 12.4 Podiatrist Physics.

When you are standing barefoot and still in a room of your house or apartment, what are the nature and source of the force you feel on the bottom of your feet?

How does that force differ from your weight?

We have all heard about the law of universal gravitation. Describe exactly what part or parts of your body the Earth's force of gravity, as specified in the law of universal gravitation, is acting upon. How is this force or these forces related to your weight?

■Q 12.5 Choosing Tacklers Wisely.

A quarterback weighs 220 lb (100 kg). He has just received the ball and is trying to pass when he sees two opposing players who have broken through the line and are moving toward him. He remembers that one of the players is his weight and has only average running speed.

The other player can run 20% faster, but weighs only 184 lb (83.3 kg). Which of these two players should the quarterback try to avoid? Who can tackle harder and do more damage? Explain carefully your answer.

Q 12.6 Egg Energy.

Imagine spinning a raw egg as fast you can and quickly making it come to a complete stop by gently pressing on the top of it with one of your fingertips (Figure 12-5).

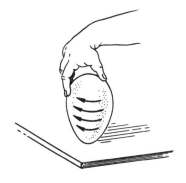

As you quickly withdraw your finger, what does the egg do? How can this be explained?

Figure 12-5

◢**A** 12.1 Log Lifting Contest.

This problem is best considered from the point of view of a rotation about the center of mass. For such a 10 ft long log, the center of mass must be at 5 ft from either end. When the three persons lift the log, all parts of it must be lifted straight upward at the same time. That way, it remains horizontal. This means the log does not rotate about its center of mass.

If that condition is to be met, then the moment about the center of mass produced by the lone person at one end of the log must balance the moment about the center of mass produced by the other two persons (Figure 12-6).

If we take D as the distance from the end of the log to where the two persons exert their lifting force, we must have 2 x 120 x (5 − D) = 60 x 5. Solving this equation for D, we get D=3.75 ft.

◢**A** 12.2 Science Tips for Boaters.

This situation with the boat actually did happen to the author. He tried repeatedly to lift and push on the boat's bow, but could not budge it at all. Then he remembered a problem in physics, where a bird that would land on a wire

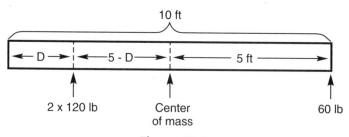

Figure 12-6

Figure 12-7

strung tightly between poles could break the wire under the very great tension introduced by the small weight of the bird (Figure 12-7).

If he could tie a line from the bow of the boat back to the piling, make it very tight, and then pull upward, he could produce very large forces of tension in the line, and it would in turn pull the boat out and off the sand beach.

Sure enough, when he did this, the boat would move out 6 or 7 in; then he would retighten the line, lift it again, and it would move another 6 or 7 in. By repeating this process several times, the boat eventually slid off the sand and into deep enough water to float it. He then was able to return to his marina, get home in time, and catch his afternoon airplane.

For any force acting on a rope or wire stretched tightly between two points, and for small angles, the component of the tension perpendicular to the original line through which the wire passed is given by the force applied perpendicularly to the wire divided by the sine of the angle formed by the wire in its new position and the original line.

Since the force that must be balanced is due to components from both sides of the place where this force is being applied, the equation for the tension, T, is given by $T = (F/2)/\sin \theta$. Since the angle θ is very small, the $\sin \theta$ is approximately equal to θ, when expressed in radians. Thus, if we know how far we lift the line, and if we know the distance from the center point where it was lifted to the tied end of the line, we can find that angle.

In the case of the boat, the line was about 15 ft from

the center point where it was lifted to where it was tied (half of the distance from the bow and to the piling). The force applied was about 150 lb and the amount lifted each time was about 1 ft. Thus, each time the line was lifted, the tension in the line, and therefore the pull on the boat, was about (150 lb/2)/(1/15). This was a force of about 1,100 lb pulling the boat off the sand.

The principle of a line under tension allowed the boater to apply a force of only 150 lb, but apply a pull of 1,100 lb. That was enough to pull the 4,000 lb boat off the sand and into deeper water.

▬A 12.3 To Brake or Not to Brake.

This item illustrates a very important aspect of motion. When you throw an object upward, we know that it must stop at the top of its motion in order to reverse direction and return to the ground. But stopping means that its speed is zero, not its acceleration.

In the case of a car moving up a 30° incline, there is a constant force downward along the incline given by the mass of the car times its acceleration along the incline. That acceleration is just g times the sine of the angle of incline, in this case 30°. Since the sine of 30° is 0.5, the acceleration down the incline is one-half g, or 4.9 meters/square second (m/s^2).

When the car comes to a stop it is still accelerating down the incline by this amount. Thus when you put your foot on the brake pedal you prevent the car from doing what it would naturally do, that is, reverse its direction and begin to speed up down the incline. You actually experience 1/2 g of force even though the speedometer reads zero at that instant.

In the case of the car moving along a level road, there is no force along the road except what is produced by friction. That is why the car is slowing down. When the car comes to a stop, there is no force acting on it along the road; therefore, when the speedometer reads zero and you put your foot on the brake pedal, you experience no force whatsoever along that horizontal direction.

◼A 12.4 Podiatrist Physics.

The force you feel on the bottom of your feet is not your weight. It is true, however, that this force has the same magnitude as your weight, but opposite in direction. The force pulling down on you, which we often call our weight, is a consequence of the law of universal gravitation. The *law of universal gravitation* states that the force acting between any two mass particles is proportional to the product of those masses and inversely proportional to the square of the distance between them.

To find the force between the earth and your body, we would need to calculate that force between every single particle of your body and every single particle of the earth, and find the sum of all of those forces, even taking into account their various directions. You can imagine how impossible this task would be the way it is described here.

This was the problem faced by Isaac Newton when he was trying to understand gravitation. To solve this problem of summing all of these forces, Newton invented a new kind of mathematics. It is called the *integral calculus.* And by using such calculus, it is relatively easy to find sums of the kind just described.

The force of gravity is this sum of forces, which is your weight. But what you experience is quite complex. Your muscles and bones all provide internal forces which prevent the particles of your body from collapsing into a thin pool on the floor. The sum of those forces, however, is transmitted to the bottom of your feet, which push on the floor. The floor pushes back upward on your feet, so that you do not fall through the floor.

These forces of interaction between the floor and your feet are actually electrical in nature. The electrons in atoms and molecules of your feet are outermost, as are the electrons in the floor. Those electrons, being pushed close together, repel, and through their repulsion, your feet experience the force of the floor pushing on them.

▪A 12.5 Choosing Tacklers Wisely.

The two opposing players have masses of 100 kg and 83.3 kg. If the heavier of the two men moves toward the quarterback at a speed v, then the lighter, but faster, player moves at 1.2v. Assume that the quarterback is standing still when he is tackled. The heavier player has a momentum of mv=100v. The lighter player has a momentum of (0.833 m)(1.2v)=mv. Thus, their momenta are the same.

In terms of momentum they hit equally hard. But what about kinetic energy? For the larger player, it is 1/2 mv²=(1/2)(100v²), or 50v². For the smaller player, it is (1/2)(83.3)(1.2v²) = 60v². Thus if the quarterback is hit by the smaller, faster player, the "damage," in terms of kinetic energy that must be dissipated, is 20% greater.

The quarterback should therefore try to avoid the smaller, faster player.

▪A 12.6 Egg Energy.

As you touch the outside of the egg and quickly remove your finger, the egg shell stops rotating but the suspended liquid contents of the egg continue to spin. This is because of *inertia* (objects in motion continue in that motion until an external force is applied). As the contents apply frictional forces to the inside of the egg shell, the shell begins to rotate again. Finally, the egg is rotating almost as rapidly as it was before you placed your finger on it to stop the motion. This is a good way to tell a raw egg from one that is hard-boiled.

For Further Reading, Research, or Study

Culotta, E. "Mass Appeal," *Science World,* vol. 49, no. 4 (Oct. 23, 1992), pp. 18–21.

This article looks at paradoxes and problems involving forces and mass. It provides a variety of interesting situations for problem solving or research.

Koger, D. "Highway." *Science World,* vol. 49, no. 5 (Nov. 6, 1992), pp. 10–13.

This article shows how the laws of physics are used to piece together the sequence of events of car crashes. It is an excellent example of how physics can be used to solve real problems.

CHAPTER 13

DARING DIMENSIONAL DIFFICULTIES

DIMENSIONS AND DENSITY can offer interesting challenges. Aluminum foil is quite thin; as you work on Q13.2, measure its thickness with a micrometer caliper. Check out some "mil" thicknesses advertised on trash bags. Quiz items seldom have one solution. There are many ways of getting a result, and interpretations can be widely varied, depending upon your knowledge and your creativity. This chapter concludes our quiz.

Use what you have learned to investigate what you do not understand and approach difficult problems with skepticism, questions, and your understanding of basic science.

■Q 13.1 More Coffee?

The illustration in Figure 13-1 shows two coffeepots placed on a level tabletop on Earth. They are both cylindrical in shape and have the same cross-sectional area. Which coffeepot would hold more coffee? Explain your answer.

■Q 13.2 Curses, Foiled Again.

Aluminum has a density of 2.70 grams/cubic centimeter (g/cm^3). A sheet of aluminum foil measures 50 cm by 120 cm.

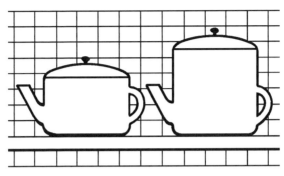

Figure 13-1

When the foil is crunched into a tight ball and placed on a balance, you find that it has a mass of 81 g. What is the thickness of the aluminum foil?

◾Q 13.3 Where's the Sugar?

Suppose that you have 5 sugar cubes, which measure 0.6 in on an edge (1.52 cm). Each cube has a mass of 3.68 grams (g). These cubes of sugar are dissolved in 100 cm³ of water. How does the level of water in the beaker compare with what it would have been if you had added 5 cubes of copper of the same size that sank to the bottom?

What is the volume of the sugar water solution? What is its density? Explain how you arrived at your answers, and what you believe must be happening.

◾Q 13.4 My Building Is 40 Barometers High?

A teacher wants to test a student's understanding of physics. She therefore asks the following question: "How can you use a mercury barometer to find the height of a building?" (Figure 13-2).

The student responds by giving four ways that the barometer can be used to find the height of the building, some rather creative. Can you think of what this student

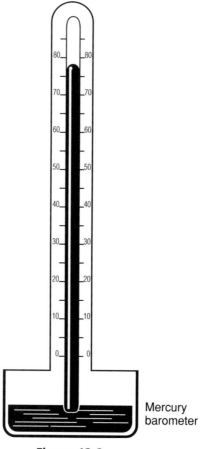

Figure 13-2

said to the teacher? (Note: This is a classic item that has been around for many years.)

A 13.1 More Coffee?

This is not just a trick question. It tests one's understanding of *Pascal's law*, that liquid pressures are applied in all directions in the liquid. It also tests your observational and analytical skills somewhat.

You must recognize that the spouts are at the same level. Then you must recognize that liquids in the two pots will move under pressures to the same levels because any excess will spill out of the spouts. The two pots therefore hold the same amount of coffee.

▪A 13.2 Curses, Foiled Again.

Since density is mass per unit of volume, we can set the density, 2.70 g/cm³, equal to the mass, 81 g, divided by the volume. But the volume is not known. We do know that the foil has an area of 120 cm x 50 cm, or 6,000 cm². This area times the thickness, T, gives the volume of the foil.

Thus we can write the equation, T = 81 g/16,200 g/cm, or T = 0.005 cm. This is, of course, 0.05 mm, the thickness of the aluminum foil.

▪A 13.3 Where's the Sugar?

When you dissolve the 5 sugar cubes in 100 cm³ of warm water, the water level rises by 11 cm³. (Try this yourself.) Yet the sugar cubes each have a volume of 3.51 cm³, or for 5 cubes a total of 17.6 cm³. You might have expected the volume to increase to 117.6 cm³. Since you have added 18.4 g of sugar to the 100 g of water, the mass is now 118.4 g, with a volume of 111 cm³. The density has gone from 1.0 g/cm³ to 1.07 g/cm³.

But when you place 5 cubes of copper metal of the same size as these sugar cubes in the water, the water level rises by 17.6 cm³. The copper cubes do not dissolve. Now, what must happen to sugar as it dissolves? There is some 6.6 cm³ of volume that is not accounted for.

Somehow, the sugar molecules must occupy space in between water molecules, and the water molecules and sugar molecules must be closer together than the original water molecules were.

■A 13.4 My Building Is 40 Barometers High?

This is a very old and classic item in physics. The author first heard it from Dr. Alexander Calandra in the 1960s. The obvious solution is to measure the barometric pressure at the base of the building, go to the top of the building and measure it again, and use the knowledge of pressure versus altitude to arrive at the height of the building.

But the creative student sees other solutions. A second solution is to take the barometer to the top of the building, drop it from rest, then, using a stopwatch, determine how long it takes to fall to the ground. From that time measurement and the value of g, the equation $d=(1/2)gt^2$ gives the height, d, of the building.

Another answer would be to stand the barometer up at a location some distance away from the building so that the barometer's shadow coincided with the tip of the building's shadow. This would form two similar triangles, from which, with the distance from the base of the building to the barometer, from the barometer to the end of the shadow, and with the height of the barometer, the building's height could be found using proportions.

But the most creative solution was for the student to take the barometer into the building, locate the building superintendent, and say, "If you tell me the height of this building, I will give you this barometer."

For Further Reading, Research, or Study

Freedman, W. "The Expansion Rate and Size of the Universe," *Scientific American,* vol. 267, no. 5. (Nov. 1992), p. 54.

This article describes how astronomers have improved estimates of the expansion rate for the universe. This is done by measuring the size of the entire universe with a variety of new techniques.

Lippy, J., and Palder, E. *Modern Chemical Magic* (Hollywood, Calif.: Angriff Press, 1987), chap. 13.

This little book describes over 50 tricks that can be done with chemicals. The science involved is interesting and could lead to good research projects for students.

INDEX

Bill G. Aldridge has been executive director of the National Science Teachers Association (NSTA) since 1980. His academic degrees include a master's degree in physics and a master's degree in educational evaluation from the University of Kansas, as well as a master's degree in science education from Harvard University. He taught high school physics and math for six years and college physics for seventeen years. Among his numerous publications are five textbooks and nine monographs. As director of the NSTA, the largest science organization in the world, he has worked with the U.S. Congress and with government agencies to design support programs for science education. Currently, he is heading a major national reform of science education called Scope, Sequence, and Coordination of Secondary School Science.